LINCOLN
AND THE IRISH

LINCOLN
AND THE IRISH

The Untold Story of How the Irish Helped
Abraham Lincoln Save the Union

NIALL O'DOWD

Skyhorse Publishing

Skyhorse Publishing books may be purchased in bulk at special discounts for sales promotion, corporate gifts, fund-raising, or educational purposes. Special editions can also be created to specifications. For details, contact the Special Sales Department, Skyhorse Publishing, 307 West 36th Street, 11th Floor, New York, NY 10018 or info@skyhorsepublishing.com.

Skyhorse® and Skyhorse Publishing® are registered trademarks of Skyhorse Publishing, Inc.®, a Delaware corporation.

Visit our website at www.skyhorsepublishing.com.

10 9 8 7 6 5 4 3 2 1

Library of Congress Cataloging-in-Publication Data is available on file.

Cover design by Brian Peterson

ISBN: 978-1-5107-3634-4
Ebook ISBN: 978-1-5107-3635-1

Printed the United States of America

TABLE OF CONTENTS

To Debbie, for all your love

ACKNOWLEDGMENTS

Let me start where it all begins, with family and friends, co-workers, editors, proofreaders, sales staff at Irish Voice, Irish Central, Irish America, and Irish Studio.

To believers, too numerous to mention.

To Dermot McEvoy, for outstanding editing and insights and introductions.

To Michael Campbell at Skyhorse, for initiative, advice, and counsel.

To 40 million Irish Americans, for a wonderful community that has always given back to me.

To Damian Shiels, whose outstanding writing about the Civil War Irish first grabbed my attention.

To Jim McManus, Civil War Irish expert, for invaluable research and information.

To Abraham Lincoln, for saving democracy.

To the Irish, for helping him.

Beir Bua Sibh Go Leir

"Write What Should Not Be Forgotten"

"Write what should not be forgotten," advises Chilean American author Isabel Allende. With that in mind, I began this book about how the Irish were a huge part of Abraham Lincoln's life and successes.

There have been 15,000 books written about Abraham Lincoln, more than on anyone in history, bar Jesus Christ. This is the only one that focuses specifically on the Lincoln-Irish connection. There have been many books on the Irish and the Civil War, but not specifically on Lincoln and his relationship with them.

It has been a remarkable omission.

Lincoln's rise coincided with the one million famine-tossed Irish flooding to America's shores, when the population of the US was only 23 million. 150,000 Irish fought for his Union. Without them, he would almost certainly have lost.

As the war news turned against them, the Confederates mounted desperate attempts to stop the Union from recruiting in Ireland in order to try and level the battlefield. They knew how important those Irish soldiers were.

Only in the first World War did more Irish ever fight for a cause together, and yet for too long there has been silence and minimal acknowledgment. Selective amnesia has occurred not just in America but in Ireland, about the men and women (yes, there were women) from Ireland who fought in the Civil War and supported Lincoln.

The role of the 25,000 who fought for the Confederacy has to be acknowledged too, as well as the many pro-slavery Irish clerics and their flocks.

But the Irish were everywhere in Lincoln's life, and not just as warriors. They nannied his kids, comforted his distressed wife, and Irish patriot Robert Emmet informed his political passion. He sang their songs, repeated their jokes, imitated their accents, and even came within minutes of fighting a duel with an Irish political opponent, which he later admitted was one of the lowest times of his life.

Once he got to the White House, he surrounded himself with so many Irish that there were dark rumblings in writings from other staff that he was surrounded by a Hibernian clique. Lincoln paid no attention. There was deep ambivalence in the relationship at the beginning. Lincoln was a Republican, a party that had a deep anti-Irish Catholic core because of the Know-Nothing influence. At first, this did not endear many Irish to him.

The Irish were, for obvious reasons, fighting hard against the nativists, who were intent on stopping the Irish from voting by using physical violence against them. In August 1855 during the "Bloody Monday" Louisville riots, up to 100 Irish were killed including some who were burned alive.

But Lincoln made it clear he had no truck with the Know–Nothings, and great leaders like Archbishop Hughes, General Thomas Francis Meagher, and General Michael Corcoran stood up and provided the needed leadership in their community by supporting him. Hughes ran up the Stars and Stripes over old St. Patrick's Cathedral while Meagher and Corcoran recruited armies.

Ending slavery was never their most important task, as they saw it. It was safeguarding their own beleaguered community first, though Meagher and Corcoran spoke strongly against slavery. Meagher even called for all blacks to be allowed vote, heresy even among some Lincoln backers.

The Irish-black relationship included large numbers of intermarriages, and was generally far more complicated than has often been portrayed. Democrats played on fears of Irish-black miscegenation, which they lied was approved by Lincoln, to drive the Irish away from the president in the 1864 election.

There were also deep tensions with Lincoln's generals, as many believed the Irish brigades were being used as cannon fodder, given their fatality rates.

Yet in the end, he plainly liked the Irish. And the Irish loved America, and resented deeply the attempt of the South to secede from it.

Unlike so many others, such as his wife and his law partner, Lincoln never spoke ill of them even in private correspondence. He had remarkably advanced views on emigration and its benefits that would shame the Know-Nothings of today.

Why is Lincoln such a fascinating topic? Perhaps because unlike Washington, to who he is most often compared, he was a man in full. Washington still feels as remote as the alabaster statue he is so often portrayed as.

Lincoln seems eternally modern; his depressions, his decidedly stormy marriage, his self-doubt, his failures, and his tragic death, coming soon after his greatest success.

But above all, there is that extraordinary vision and empathy, the ability to see what his own generals and cabinet urging compromise could not see—that the very future of democracy was on the line, that there could be no compromise on slavery. He knew that groups like the Irish were not to be despised, but brought on board in the great struggle.

He was the master mariner in waters that had never been navigated by any president, but he would need the help of the Irish and others to safely reach the shore.

Coming from a poor and underprivileged background, he understood the Irish only too well. Like him they were magnificent fighters, never better than at Gettysburg, where they played a major role in the outcome of one of the most significant battles ever.

Their story should be America's story, but their voices only linger faintly. Their role is ignored by many contemporary historians, including Ken Burns with his landmark PBS series *The Civil War*. Eminent historian Gabor S. Boritt of Gettysburg College asked a key question about the Burns series: where are the voices of the immigrant soldiers (Irish, German, etc.) who made up 25 percent of the Union Army? Where indeed.

But they were heard by Lincoln. He gave them credit and acknowledgment for what they accomplished but also held them up to criticism and punishment when they fell short, as in the abysmal draft riots, the worst moment in Irish-American history.

We should never forget that the Irish helped Lincoln save democracy and end slavery. Hopefully, this book will play a part in ensuring that one of the most important stories in the history of the Irish is not forgotten.

CHAPTER ONE

Scoop of the Century

In the misty early morning of Wednesday, April 26, 1865, three men in a small rowing boat set out from Crookhaven, a tiny fishing village in County Cork, Ireland, to intercept the mail steamer *Marseilles*.

The *Marseilles* had rendezvoused off the Cork coast and picked up canisters of US mail from the *Teutonia*, a Hamburg-bound ship via Southampton that had left New York twelve days earlier. The *Teutonia* had loomed into view off the Irish coast at 8:00 a.m. It was carrying the latest news from America.

The three men, the lookout who had first sighted the ship from a rocky outcrop called Brow Head, and the men on the mail ship itself, were all paid employees of Paul Julius Reuter, a dynamic newspaperman and German immigrant who was determined to have the news first, whatever it took. His name would become a household one soon enough because of the events of that day.

Like all successful men and women of business, Reuter saw an opportunity and took it. In his case, it was building a private telegraph line from Cork City to Crookhaven, the first point of land close enough for a ship from America to be intercepted. The other news services would wait until the ship pulled into Cobh, then called

Queenstown, some twenty-five miles further up the coast. Time was money, and Reuter was in a hurry.

At the time, it took about twelve days by steamship to cross the Atlantic. Telegraph lines west from London stopped at County Cork. In America, no working lines yet crossed the Atlantic though there had been many attempts.

Thus, in April 1865 any news from the United States would first come from the mail boat picking up from the transatlantic steamer in the waters off County Cork, the closest landfall, and would then be quickly routed to London and Europe through the Cork City cable office.

If Abraham Lincoln had died just one year later the news would have reached Europe almost immediately, as the first working transatlantic telegraph cable would make land at Valentia Island off Kerry. In 1866. It could handle eight words per minute.

The *Marseilles* this day would carry the biggest story of the century—the assassination of American president Abraham Lincoln. Though he had been shot on April 14 and America was ablaze with the news and the successful hunt for the assassin, Europe remained blissfully unaware until twelve days later.

The main news in the *London Evening Standard* was the celebration and events around the tercentenary of the birth of William Shakespeare and the death of the elder brother of the Czar of Russia.

That was about to change.

The key man was James "Tugboat" McLean, Reuter's man in New York.

McLean was Reuter's go-getting correspondent, in those days called an agent. He was later called "Tugboat" because his news of Lincoln's death almost came too late to put aboard the *Teutonia*. He pursued the ship on a tugboat and threw the watertight canisters containing his historic report aboard.

Some claim it was a different man than McLean, a fellow German James Hecksher, a friend and New York employee of Reuter's, who pursued the tugboat and threw the canisters on board.

Onward the ship sailed across the wide ocean, bearing its message of profound importance and impact, before transferring the news canisters to the *Marseilles*. When that ship came in sight of Irish shores, the purser lowered the canisters and dropped them in the water as the ship drew close to the three men who had rowed out. They snagged them with nets on long poles like huge fishing nets.

They rowed back to Crookhaven, where the telegraph operator broke open the canisters and read their sensational import. Soon, the telegraph lines between remote Cork and the great cities of Europe began a chatter that soon built to a frenzy. By the noon bulletin, hours before his rivals, Reuter broke the news that shocked the world. It was so shocking that many thought it a hoax, and Reuter's reputation was on the line. A few hours later, it was confirmed.

The Great Emancipator Abraham Lincoln was dead.

Reuter's news hit Britain and Ireland like a thunderbolt.

"The blow is sudden, horrible, irretrievable," wrote the *London Evening Standard*. "Never, since the death of Henry IV [of France] by the hand of Ravaillac—never, perhaps, since the assassination of Caesar—has a murder been committed more momentous in its bearing upon the times."

England wept, Ireland too. Lincoln had been a hero to so many. Grown men cried openly. American consulates were besieged. Church groups, anti-slavery societies, labor groups, chambers of commerce were devastated. Historian Richard Carwardine described that there were some Confederate supporters gloating on the floor of the Liverpool Stock Exchange. One trader cheered, but was thrown out by another who said, "You incarnate fiend, you have the heart of an assassin yourself!"

A "cult of Lincoln," in the words of George Bernard Shaw, sprung up in Britain after his death and arguably has continued ever since. In 1920, a statue of Lincoln sculpted by Irish-born sculptor Augustus Saint-Gaudens was unveiled in Parliament Square, entitled "Lincoln the Man." Prime Minister David Lloyd was present. Civil War veterans attended.

The cult spread to Russia, where forty-five years later Leo Tolstoy stated, "The greatness of Napoleon, Caesar, or Washington is only moonlight by the sun of Lincoln." He predicted that "his example is universal and will last thousands of years."

Reuter was forever famous for bearing the news. Hollywood even came out with the film *A Dispatch from Reuter's* in 1940, starring Edward G. Robinson as Reuter, about the events around getting the Lincoln story first.

The news of Abe Lincoln's death first came ashore in Ireland. It would be the last connection between a legendary president and a country whose people had played a huge role in his life. Lincoln's relationship with the Irish was an extraordinary story, too.

When the Kentucky backwoods rail splitter set out on his extraordinary political journey, he encountered the Irish at every step. His rise coincided with the greatest ever inward migration of a people, the million Irish fleeing the Famine. In a country of just twenty-three million, the arrival of the Irish had an immense impact.

He knew them, fought them, embraced them, cursed them, thanked them profusely, and kissed their flag. He gathered a Hibernian cabal around him in the White House and was criticized for so doing. It is highly unlikely he could have won the most important war ever fought for the future of democracy without them. They were 150,000 strong in his army, which peaked at 600,000 men in late 1863. Irishmen had never fought in such numbers for their own country. The fuse was lit by the Civil War and in the tide of battle they were led by their heroes like Thomas Francis Meagher and Michael Corcoran.

Lincoln appeared to regard the Irish with a benign demeanor most of the time. Even in his most private writings, he exhibited none of the hatred towards them that many of his contemporaries, including his wife and law partner, did. He told Irish jokes, very mild in nature. The old Irish doorman Edward McManus at the White House was said to be the only person who could make him laugh with his funny Irish stories.

His children were cared for by them. He wined and dined their heroes, such as Thomas Francis Meagher and Michael Corcoran, and showed up at a Fighting 69th camp and kissed the Irish flag. Francis Burke, the man who drove him to Ford's Theatre that dreadful night, was Irish, as was his valet Charlie Forbes, the last man to speak to the assassin Booth before he killed the president.

James O'Beirne and Edward Doherty, two men who were among the leaders who tracked down his killer, were Irish as well. General Philip Sheridan, who ended the war a folk hero on the Union side, had family direct from Cavan and was either born there himself, or more likely at sea on the voyage over.

When it came to the Irish, Abraham Lincoln was no stranger.

CHAPTER TWO

Mary and Abe and Their Irish Maids

M ary Todd Lincoln was of solid Irish stock.

Mary's paternal great-grandfather, David Levi Todd, was born in County Longford, Ireland, and came to America, via Pennsylvania, to Kentucky. Another great-grandfather, Andrew Porter, was also of Irish stock, the son of an Irish immigrant to New Hampshire and later Pennsylvania. Abraham Lincoln was primarily of English descent, though there was some Scots-Irish in his roots, namely a McLoughlin and a McKinley.

Mary Todd moved to Springfield, Illinois, from Kentucky in 1839, at the age of twenty-one. She went in order to escape her stepmother, live with her sister Elizabeth, and begin the search for a husband. Springfield had become the state capitol and was overrun with men fastening down political and lobbying careers, as well as a plethora of chancers, fakers, hustlers, and some do-gooders.

Women were in short supply, which suited Mary Todd. Back then, a woman's prospects in life depended on what kind of marriage she made, not on her own abilities. Mary was determined to meet the right match.

She had "a well-rounded face, rich dark-brown hair and bluish-grey eyes," according to Lincoln's law partner William Herndon, who was no fan. She spoke fluent French and had a long and distinguished ancestral line. Mary was about five foot two and weighed about 130 pounds, though in later years she would gain weight.

She and Lincoln became acquainted at a cotillion. "Who is that man?" is what Mary said in reaction to seeing for the first time the long, gangly figure of the country lawyer and budding politician. Her reaction to seeing Lincoln was recorded by Mary's niece, Katherine Helm.

Later at the cotillion, Abraham Lincoln came over and said, "Miss Todd, I want to dance with you in the worst way." They had a stormy courtship, a presentiment of what was to come. In the fall of 1842, the couple decided to be married, despite her family's concern about his rough-hewn background. Her sister Elizabeth, who had brought her to Springfield, had married well to Ninian Edwards, the son of a former governor, and tried to break up the match to the backwoodsman.

She wrote, "I warned Mary that she and Mr. Lincoln were not suitable. Mr. Edwards and myself believed that they were different in nature and education and raising."

When Mary announced their wedding would go ahead, her sister exploded. Elizabeth "with an outburst, gave Mary a good scolding, saying to her vehemently 'Do not forget you're a Todd,'" Mary's other sister, Frances, remembers.

Even his accent and voice were a drawback, a country bumpkin mixture of Indiana and Kentucky and a high-pitched voice at odds with his great hulking figure.

Speaking of his looks, it was bad enough her sister thought she was marrying beneath herself in the incredibly class-conscious mentality of the time, but then there was Mr. Lincoln's visage and presentation.

When he became a national contender, Lincoln was memorably described in the *Houston Telegraph* as "the leanest, lankiest, most ungainly mass of legs, arms, and hatchet face ever strung upon a single frame. He has most unwarrantably abused the privilege which all politicians have of being ugly."

In an era before photographs, such descriptions were damning. An anti-Lincoln refrain ended with the lines "Don't for God's sake show his picture."

A reporter for *The Amboy Times* who went to hear Lincoln speak was hardly flattering about his appearance, but he found his two-hour speech mesmerizing.

"He is about six feet high, crooked-legged, stoop shouldered, spare built, and anything but handsome in the face. It is plain that nature took but little trouble in fashioning his outer man, but a gem may be encased in a rude casket."

Lincoln realized his best bet lay in a flattering photograph, the exciting new technology. He was perfectly aware his ungainly body, oversized hands, hard-edged and lined face, and physical presence at six foot four (in an era where the average male height was five foot seven) could be off-putting. When he launched his presidential bid, he turned to Irish photographer Matthew Brady, the Annie Leibowitz of his day.

Brady claimed he was born near Lake George in upstate New York in 1822. No birth certificate or any kind of documentation has been found to link his birth to New York State. In fact, an 1855 New York census lists Brady's place of birth as Ireland, as do an 1860 census and Brady's own 1863 draft records. His parents, Andrew and Julia, were Irish immigrants. Given the suspicions and prejudice about Irish Catholic immigrants, Brady may have preferred to claim American birth.

He grew up in Saratoga Springs and became fascinated with the new art of photography, eventually opening his own studios in New York City. He became known as the best photographer in town at a time when the craft was in its infancy and the rich were clamoring for their likenesses to be created.

Brady had poor eyesight and hired others to take most of his photographs, but he "conceptualized images, arranged the sitters, and oversaw the production of pictures." Plus, according to *The New York Times*, Brady was "not averse to certain forms of retouching"; an early Photoshop genius, in point of fact.

The photograph he took of the future president, which coincided with Lincoln's breakthrough speech at the Cooper Union in February 1860, flattered his subject greatly. Brady bathed Lincoln's face in light to hide the hard edges and wrinkled, sallow skin. He told him to curl up his fingers to hide the sheer length of his hands. Brady "artificially enlarged" Lincoln's collar so his gangling neck would look more proportional.

Lincoln loved it, later saying, "Brady and the Cooper Institute made me President." In all, Brady and his team took thirty photographs of him. Those pictures shaped his legacy of being the first American president made truly accessible by photographs.

Whatever he looked like, Mary Todd was in love, as was her beau Abe with her. The wedding ring Lincoln bought her had an inscription that read "A.L. to Mary, Nov. 4, 1842. Love is Eternal."

Abraham Lincoln and Mary Todd were married at her older sister Elizabeth's home on Friday evening, November 4, 1842. She wore her sister's white satin dress and a pearl necklace. About thirty relatives and friends attended the ceremony. It rained.

In 1844, after living in lodgings in Springfield, they moved to 8th Street and Jackson, as their son Robert, who had been born the previous August, grew older. Mary loved her new home. "The little home was painted white and had green shutters. It was sweet and fresh, and Mary loved it. She was exquisitely dainty, and her house was a reflection of herself, everything in good taste and in perfect order," a friend reported.

As the family expanded, there was a need for maids. Lincoln's improved financial circumstances meant that help could be hired. Many at the time came straight off the boats from Ireland and Germany. Vere Foster, an agent for the Women's Protective Emigration Society in New York, was constantly being petitioned to send young girls into service in Illinois. She eventually sent 700, most of them Irish and German.

These young women found homes in Springfield, as well as other Illinois towns. Several at various times were hired by the Lincolns.

Despite her own heritage, Mary Todd Lincoln disliked the Irish and was thought to favor the Know-Nothings, the virulently anti-Irish Catholic grouping that split her husband's Whig party. She wrote to a friend in Kentucky, "If some of you Kentuckians had to deal with the Wild Irish as we housekeepers are sometimes called upon to do, the South would certainly elect Fillmore (who was favorable to Know-Nothings) the next time." Lincoln, on the other hand, made clear he was not against the Irish. After all, he was surrounded by them as domestic help at home, and many historians believe the help shielded him from the worst of his wife's tantrum excesses.

The women hired were mostly young and single. Their pay was $1.00 to $1.50 a week. (In contrast, Lincoln made up to $2,500 a year as a lawyer.) The work was exhausting—laundering, emptying chamber pots, and looking after four rambunctious boys who were poorly disciplined by their parents to begin with. Later, Mary Todd Lincoln would be called "Hellcat" as a nickname in the White House. She was just as hard on her Irish maids.

Despite her Irish heritage, Mary Todd Lincoln held a deep grudge against the Irish and constantly had problems with her Irish maids while raising her children in Springfield. Catherine Gordon, from Ireland, was named as living in the household in the 1850 census. She was likely the one who enraged Mary Todd Lincoln by leaving her window open so boyfriends could enter. Ten years later, Mary Johnson, also from Ireland, was in situ for the census. Mary was likely the one that Abe Lincoln paid to put up with his wife's tirades, an extra dollar a week slipped to her in order to placate and manage his wife.

Margaret Ryan, another Irish native, claimed she lived at the Lincoln household until 1860 and witnessed Mary hitting her husband and chasing him out of the house on several occasions. She stated all this in an interview with Jesse Weik, who helped William Herndon, Lincoln's law partner, write his definitive biography of Lincoln. Herndon hated Mary Todd Lincoln, and as a result, the

Ryan stories are hotly disputed. But there are more than enough stories told by disparate figures over her lifetime to suggest that Mary Todd Lincoln was a deeply troubled woman, a condition exacerbated by the death of three of her children.

Lincoln's niece Harriet Chapman, who worked for a time with Mary, stated she had nothing good to say about her but could talk about her uncle all day. Unpredictable outbursts and unreasonable demands was one description of Mary Todd Lincoln's behavior at the time.

Perhaps the most poignant moment of all is when Lincoln took her to an upstairs room in the White House after her grieving for her dead son Willie had sent her into a profound depression. "Mother," he said quietly to her, "You see the insane asylum yonder. You will have to go there if you cannot stop the grieving." It was a harsh choice for a woman, who had little medical expertise at the time to help treat her. It also spoke volumes for Lincoln's desperation for her to get better.

Throughout all those trying times and despite Mary Todd's scorn, Abraham Lincoln often focused on the story of the Irish who were flooding into America and sang the praise of their heroes.

CHAPTER THREE

Lincoln on Robert Emmet and the Irish Struggle

Lincoln is known to have learned Robert Emmet's speech from the dock by heart. Robert Emmet, just twenty-five, made the speech in 1803 after being sentenced to death for leading an abortive insurrection in Dublin. As a young man, Lincoln would often deliver it as a party piece for dignitaries visiting Perry County, where he lived.

Emmet's address was a necessary speech to learn for potential orators, but Lincoln seemed to have considered him a talisman. Knowing this years later, a political opponent won a surprising reprieve for a young Confederate spy.

In February 1865, Lincoln was considering an appeal to spare the boy when Delaware Senator Willard Saulsbury, who in January 1863 had called the president "a weak and imbecile man, the weakest that I ever knew in a high place," appealed for clemency.

Saulsbury played the Emmet card. He wrote, "You know I am no political friend of yours. You know I neither ask or expect any personal favor from you or your Administration . . . All I ask of you is to read the defense of this young man (Samuel B. Davis), unassisted by Counsel, compare it with the celebrated defense of Emmet, and act as the judgment and the heart of the President of the United States should act."

The death sentence was duly commuted.

Emmet continued as a lodestar. Lincoln also had direct contact with a member of the Emmet family. In 1856 at the Republican National Convention in New York, the chairman and keynote speaker at the convention was Robert Emmet, the patriot's nephew and a successful politician and judge in New York. Emmet made a passionate attack on the Democrats and their embrace of slavery and may well have influenced Lincoln.

There was one other case recounted by Henry Wilson, abolitionist and later vice president under Ulysses S. Grant, who told the story of an Irish deserter that Lincoln saved. Wilson told the story in an interview with William Herndon, Lincoln's law partner and biographer:

> I remember talking early one Sabbath morning with a wounded Irish officer who came to Washington to say that a soldier who had been sentenced to be shot in a day or two for desertion had fought bravely by his side in battle. The officer said, "Told him (Lincoln) that we had come to ask him to pardon the poor soldier." After a few moments reflection he said, "My officers tell me the good of the service demands the enforcement of the Law; but it makes my heart ache to have the poor fellows shot. I will pardon him."

Lincoln was keenly aware of world affairs despite his backwater upbringing. During the Hungarian revolution from 1847 to 1849, Congressman Lincoln, who had been elected in 1846, was one of a handful of US politicians to draft a statement in support of the Hungarian rebel Lajos Kossuth, who was seeking to break away from Austria. In the resolution, a specific reference to the Irish struggle was included. The statement was also highly critical of the British rule in Ireland, and specifically mentioned the mistreatment of two leaders of the failed 1848 Irish uprising rebels: John Mitchel, ironically a bitter opponent of Lincoln later and a supporter of slavery who settled in the South, and William Smith O'Brien, who was transported to Tasmania. The resolution reads:

> That the sympathies of this country, and the benefits of its position, should be exerted in favor of the people of every nation struggling to be free; and whilst we meet to do honor to Kossuth and Hungary, we should not fail to pour out the tribute of our praise and approbation to the patriotic efforts of the Irish, the Germans, and the French, who have unsuccessfully fought to establish in their several governments the supremacy of the people. That there is nothing in the past history of the British government, or in its present expressed policy, to encourage the belief that she will aid, in any manner, in the delivery of continental Europe from the yoke of despotism; and that her treatment of Ireland, of O'Brien, Mitchel, and other worthy patriots, forces the conclusion that she will join her efforts to the despots of Europe in suppressing every effort of the people to establish free governments, based upon the principles of true religious and civil liberty.

He also clearly liked the Irish sense of humor and bearing. Speaking about Edward Hannegan, an Indiana senator who had been double crossed for a position he thought he had been promised, Lincoln stated, "Hannegan had been a senator from Indiana six years, and, in that time, had done his state some credit, and gained some reputation for himself; but in the end, was undermined and superseded by a man who will never do either. He (Hannegan) was the son of an Irishman, with a bit of the brogue still lingering on his tongue; and with a very large share of that sprightliness and generous feeling, which generally characterize Irishmen who have had anything of a fair chance in the world. He was personally a great favorite with senators, and particularly so with Mr. Clayton, although of opposite politics."

Despite Lincoln's sympathy towards the Irish, it would be an altercation with an Irish rival—a fellow lawyer, budding politician, and remarkable leader of men in his own right—that would threaten to change the course of history years before the Civil War.

CHAPTER FOUR

Lincoln's Near Duel to the Death with an Irish Rival

James Shields is one of the most amazing Irishmen of any era. He became a US senator from three different states, a feat never again accomplished, and he was the only Union general to out think and defeat Stonewall Jackson. He also had a "man-of-mystery" image with allegations of a torrid affair with a Confederate informer. He was a hero to Irish Americans who bitterly blamed Lincoln for not keeping and promoting him as a Civil War general of the highest rank. In later life, he sought to establish Irish townships in Minnesota.

He is most famous, however, because he came within minutes of possibly taking Abraham Lincoln's life in a duel that could have changed American history forever.

Yet, there are relatively few sources on this amazing man, a County Tyrone native who came to America at the age of sixteen to join an uncle who promised him a good living. When he arrived, his namesake uncle had passed on, and he was alone.

He did not lack the fighting Irish spirit, however. An ancestor had fought at the Battle of the Boyne in 1690, ironically, against Stonewall Jackson's ancestor John Jackson. The Battle of the Boyne was the climactic moment in the war between the Catholic King

James and his Protestant rival William of Orange for the throne of England.

On the morning of June 30, 1690, King William was reconnoitering the battlefield and stopped for breakfast within range of the Catholic guns. John Jackson was with him. As William remounted, a Jacobite soldier fired twice. The first one missed. The second, however, would have killed him, but for striking John Jackson's pistol before hitting William in the shoulder, causing a minor wound.

One of the great "what ifs" of Irish history is, what would have happened if Jackson had not deflected the bullet? John Jackson saved King William's life in that battle, condemning the Shields family to eviction and hardship. Little did the ancestors know that their ancestral offspring would also meet on a battlefield, both commanding armies generations later with the future of another British colony, America, at stake.

Like all Catholics on the losing side, the Shields clan were punished for their effrontery in daring to rebel. Once extensive landowners in Antrim, they had to relocate to forsaken mountain land in Tyrone.

James Shields was born in Altmore, County Tyrone, on May 12, 1806. His father died when he was six, and his Scottish mother reared her family singlehanded.

He grew up in an Ireland where old soldiers abounded, Irish men who had fought Britain's Napoleonic wars. From them, from an early age, he learned the stagecraft of military skills and became an accomplished swordsman and shooter. His uncle, also James, came home from America for a time. A veteran of the War of Independence, he had been injured at the Battle of New Orleans.

From him, most likely, James also learned how to lead men. He received an education in the classics from a priest relative and learned to speak French from the old soldiers. He came to America unusually talented.

He put to sea for a time and rose to the rank of purser, but after an accident that badly injured him, he decided on a career as a lawyer. He also served as a soldier when on home leave from the ship.

Home from the sea, he moved to Illinois to the territorial capital called Kaskaskia and was admitted to the bar in 1832. He ran for public office soon after, winning a seat in the state legislature and moved to Vandalia, the state capital.

There he met the young Abraham Lincoln and Democratic Party veteran Stephen Douglas, two men who would go on to dominate American discourse for the most vital years in US history. Shields befriended Douglas so much that he was best man at his second wedding. He also followed him into politics as a Democrat.

It is no exaggeration to say that a man selected three times as a senator from separate states and a war hero to boot could also have been a leading presidential contender, were it not for his Irish birth.

He was described thusly in the Minnesota Historical Society Collections: "His personal appearance and manners were engaging. He was five-feet-nine inches tall, of fine figure and graceful bearing. His voice was well modulated; his speech frank, clear and resolute. He was prominent in debate and influential in council."

Another contemporary account described him as a "gallant, hot-headed bachelor from Tyrone County, Ireland."

It was clear that Shields was a hit with the ladies but also a politician on the rise, when he was elected State Auditor of Accounts in 1841, a statewide office. Soon he and Lincoln would cross paths in a near duel that, if it had gone ahead, might have changed history as surely as John Jackson blocking the bullet meant for King William did.

The near duel with Shields haunted Abraham Lincoln his entire lifetime. "If all the good things I have ever done are remembered as long and well as my scrape with Shields, it is plain I will soon be forgotten," he told James Herndon.

The genesis of the Lincoln-Shields feud was Lincoln's view that Shields was levying excessive taxation. In August of 1842, the Illinois State Bank declared bankruptcy and said it would no longer accept paper money, and gold and silver, which most ordinary citizens did not have access to, would be needed to pay debts. Shields decide to close the bank and became a target of Whig fury.

Abraham Lincoln took to the pages of the *Springfield Journal* under the pseudonym "Rebecca" to mock the Irishman Shields. It was nasty stuff, and Shields did not take to it kindly. Chiefly, Lincoln sneered at Shields's ladies' man reputation, which may also have reflected a tinge of jealousy on the part of the less-than-handsome Lincoln.

The letters were spiteful. "Dear girls, it is distressing, but I cannot marry you all. Too well I know how much you suffer; but do, do remember, it is not my fault that I am so handsome and so interesting."

Lincoln showed the letter to Mary Todd—the couple had only recently gotten back together after Lincoln had called off their earlier engagement—and she found it delightful. A few days later, without Lincoln's knowledge, Mary Todd submitted her own critique to the *Journal* under the pen name "Cathleen."

Mary Todd composed a sneering ditty, the first few lines of which ran:

Ye Jews Harp awake the auditors won
Rebecca the widow has gained Erin's son
The pride of the North from the Emerald Isle
Has been wooed and won by a woman's smile.

Shields was infuriated by the low satire. He demanded Simeon Francis, the newspaper's editor, reveal the author, which Francis surprisingly did.

Declaring it an affair of honor, Shields demanded a duel. "I have become the object of slander, vituperation and personal abuse. Only a full retraction may prevent consequences which no one will regret more than myself."

Lincoln refused to retract his remarks. He returned Shields's letter with the request that Shields rewrite it in a more "gentlemanly" fashion. Instead, Shields challenged Lincoln to a duel. It would be held in Missouri, where dueling was still legal.

Since Lincoln was challenged by Shields, he had the privilege of choosing the weapon of the duel. He chose cavalry broadswords "of the largest size."

"I didn't want the damned fellow to kill me, which I think he would have done if we had selected pistols," he later said. He was right; going back to his military upbringing in Ireland, Shields would surely have won a pistol duel.

Subsequently, Shields also exhibited great bravery in the war with Mexico and as a Civil War general. Lincoln, with his much longer reach, had chosen wisely.

The Lincoln-Shields duel is one of these "what if" moments in history. If Shields had won, history would have changed dramatically. Stephen Douglas would likely have been president, and the issue of slavery might have turned out very differently.

Luckily, Lincoln had his pick of weapon.

How heavy were the swords? In the early 1870s, Army Captain M. J. O'Rourke, an Irish-American historian and teacher of the history of the sword, in referring to cavalry swords, described them as those "ponderous blades, in wielding which they required all the strength of both [hands]."

Lincoln created conditions so favorable to him because of his towering height that he was sure that Shields would demur. He ordered "a plank ten feet long, and from nine to twelve inches abroad, to be firmly fixed on edge, on the ground, as the line between us, which neither is to pass his foot over upon forfeit of his life."

Forced to literally toe that line, the five-foot-nine Shields had no chance against the long-limbed Lincoln swinging a mighty broadsword. Surely Shields would concede?

But even that condition, which likely meant certain death, was still not enough to deter Shields, who certainly did not lack bravery. So on September 22, 1842, Shields left his home state, where a duel was a criminal act, and headed for Bloody Island, Missouri, where Lincoln awaited him. It was a "to be a kill or be killed" standoff.

They advanced to the field where the score was to be settled once and for all. Both men were surrounded by seconds, close friends to ensure a fair fight. It was clear the rival supporters wished for a settlement.

At the last moment, the seconds intervened and cobbled together a Lincoln apology that satisfied both parties, so the duel was called off. The duelers left the field in much better form than when they arrived, laughing and talking. Subsequently, the men became friends.

Lincoln never forgot the incident, which troubled him deeply the rest of his life. In a letter written about the aftermath of the incident on December 9, 1865, Mary Todd Lincoln wrote that an army officer during a receiving line at the White House asked her husband, "Is it true . . . that you once went out, to fight a duel and all for the sake of the lady by your side?"

Lincoln replied, "I do not deny it, but if you desire my friendship, you will never mention it again."

However, it was not the end of the Shields-Lincoln relationship. The two men would soon enough be comrades in arms against the South in yet another twist of fate. Shields was set to become a war hero; he was a senator from three different states, had a record never surpassed, and success that was a rallying point for the Irish in the Union Army. He was also a strong proponent of Irish resettlement in the Midwest.

But all that was in the future. In the present, the American political landscape was rearranging itself, and a rising Lincoln and the newly arrived Irish found themselves at the center of it.

CHAPTER FIVE

Lincoln's New Party, Anti-Irish and Anti-Slavery

By 1856, the Whig party Lincoln belonged to had destroyed itself over slavery and the violence of the Know-Nothings, an extremist group of nativists with a deep hatred of immigrants and Catholics that existed as an independent force but who were much closer to the Whigs and later the new Republican Party.

Lincoln by then was well steeped in Irish culture, history, and politics. It was one reason he would have no truck with the Nativists and the Know-Nothings. His favorite ballad as a young man was titled "The Lament of the Irish Emigrant," set to music. It is an elegy for a young girl, Mary, who died of starvation during the Famine. We also know Lincoln contributed $10 to Famine relief, the equivalent of $500 today.

Lincoln's contribution came after a mass meeting in Washington to raise money for Ireland. He urged that every American state should follow suit. The Washington meeting was attended by many politicians.

During the meeting, letters were read from Ireland, including one from the women of Dunmanway in County Cork. It was addressed to the Ladies of America. It said, "Oh that our American sisters could see the laborers on our roads, able-bodied men, scarcely clad, famished with hunger, with despair in their once-cheerful faces, staggering at their work. . . . Oh that they could see the dead father, mother, or child, lying coffinless, and hear the screams of the survivors around them, caused not by sorrow, but by the agony of hunger."

Professor Christine Kinealy, director of the Great Hunger Institute at Quinnipiac University in Connecticut, rates Lincoln's contribution to famine relief highly. "This was back in 1847, when Lincoln was only a newly elected politician to the House of Representatives. It was an insubstantial sum from an unimportant figure at the time, but it is retrospectively very interesting," the Trinity College graduate stated.

Kinealy asserts that this donation was not out of character for Lincoln, who had a lifelong rapport with the Irish.

"I suppose Lincoln always had a great affinity for the Irish and their plight. He knew and recited Robert Emmet's speech from the dock and his favorite ballad was Lady Dufferin's poem 'The Lament of the Irish Emigrant' set to music."

Perhaps it was the poignant lyrics of that song that inspired the generous donation. A verse runs:

> I thank you for the patient smile
> When your heart was fit to break,
> When the hunger pain was gnawin' there,
> And you hid it, for my sake!
> I bless you for the pleasant word,
> When your heart was sad and sore—
> O, I'm thankful you are gone, Mary,
> Where grief can't reach you more!

Lincoln didn't just absorb the maudlin side of the Irish. He also told Irish jokes, gently poking fun without any real malice.

Lincoln may also have gotten his Irish affinity from his first schoolmaster Zachariah Riney, an Irish Catholic who Lincoln subsequently held in very great respect. According to the oral history of the Rineys of Kentucky, four Riney brothers emigrated from County Kerry, Ireland, in the late 1700s. These four brothers were probably James, John, Thomas, and Jonathan, a Revolutionary War soldier. Many of the Rineys migrated to Kentucky. Thomas was the father of Zachariah Riney, the first schoolteacher of Abraham Lincoln.

Riney insisted on correct spellings but also, with the older boys, distilling sentences down so that the bare minimum of words sufficed. Some historians have credited Riney with Lincoln's uncanny ability, as with the Gettysburg Address, to distill profound thoughts into such simple sentences.

But despite the help of the much-respected Irish American schoolteacher and the immediate Irish connections through domestic help and a cultural affinity, there were deep and very strongly held differences between Lincoln and the Irish.

During his early political battles, Lincoln could often be ambivalent about them. They favored the Democrats and were hostile to his Republican party. There were many in his own party who despised them.

In the twenty years before the Civil War, four million people from Europe emigrated. It was the Irish, fleeing the Famine, who made up the largest numbers, and their massive influx right at the time that Lincoln was shaping his political career presented formidable problems to him. With an alien culture and religion, and arriving in terrible straits after the dreadful impact of the Famine, the Irish were ripe for sparking a wave of nativism.

The Know-Nothings were born and quickly became identified with the fledgling Republican Party and, by association, with Lincoln. Their aim was simple—to rid America of the despised foreigners. They believed the Irish in particular paid allegiance to the pope and not to their new country, and they made a compact to destroy them.

The intensity of the hatred of Irish immigrants can be gauged by what happened in Louisville on August 5, 1855, in Lincoln's home state where, urged on by rabble-rousing newspaper editor George Prentice, the Know-Nothing mob descended on a shanty Irish neighborhood.

Prentice called the Irish and German the "most pestilent influence of the foreign swarms," loyal to a pope he called "an inflated Italian despot who keeps people kissing his toes all day."

The bigotry, raw even for its time, of Prentice's comments inflamed the mob, who were determined to stop Irish and German Catholics from voting. What happened next became known as "Bloody Monday," with estimates ranging from twenty-two to one hundred Irish slaughtered, many as they tried to escape being burned alive.

An editorial in the *Louisville Daily Journal* entitled "Bloody Work" revisited the terrible events:

> After dusk, a row of frame houses on Main Street between Tenth and Eleventh, the property of Mr. Quinn, a well-known Irishman, was set on fire. The flames extended across the street and twelve buildings were destroyed. These houses were chiefly tenanted by Irish, and upon any of the tenants venturing out to escape the flames, they were immediately shot down. No idea could be formed on the number killed. We are advised that five men were roasted to death, having been so badly wounded by gunshot wounds that they could not escape from the burning buildings.
>
> Of all the enormities and outrages committed by the American Party (the official name for the Know-Nothings) yesterday and last night, we have not time now to write.
>
> Upon the proceedings of yesterday and last night we have no time, nor heart, now to comment. We are sickened with the very thought of the men murdered, and houses burned and pillaged, that signalized the American victory yesterday.

Similar Know-Nothing riots had taken place in Philadelphia, leaving fourteen dead and the destruction of two Catholic churches and neighborhoods. The Philadelphia Nativist Riots took place in 1844 between May 6 and 8, and July 6 and 7. The riots were the result of a rumor that Catholics were trying to remove the Bible from public schools. The connection between the Know-Nothings and the fledgling Republican Party was well known to the Irish. The paradox was that many Republicans were both nativist and anti-slavery. But hatred of Irish Catholics topped their list. In order to be a member of the Know-Nothing Party, one had to meet the following criteria: be twenty-one years of age, believe in God, be a native-born Protestant American, be raised a Protestant, and never marry a Catholic.

One Know-Nothing summarized the issue: "[In order to protect our country, we will hire only those not under] . . . the insidious policy of the Church of Rome, and [avoid] all other foreign influences against the institutions of our country, by placing in all offices . . . whether by election or appointment, none but native-born Protestant citizens." Even though the Know-Nothing Party denounced all immigrants, it especially hated Irish Catholics. Their credo was very similar to that of the Orange Order.

On August 24, 1855, in the wake of the killings in Louisville on Bloody Monday, Lincoln wrote to his close friend Joshua Speed, who had asked his opinion on the Know-Nothings. Lincoln could not have been clearer:

> I am not a Know-Nothing. That is certain. How could I be? How can anyone who abhors the oppression of negroes, be in favor of degrading classes of white people? Our progress in degeneracy appears to me to be pretty rapid. As a nation, we begin by declaring that "all men are created equal." We now practically read it "all men are created equal, except negroes." When the Know-Nothings get control, it will read "all men are created equal, except negroes, and foreigners, and Catholics." When it comes to this I should prefer emigrating to some country where they make no pretense of loving liberty—to Russia, for instance, where despotism can be taken pure, and without the base alloy of hypocrisy [sic] those and foreigners, and Catholics.

It was a remarkable stance for the time, and the total opposite of many in the new Republican Party he had just helped create. Exactly how despised the Irish were among close associates was revealed by the comments of Herndon, Lincoln's law partner and biographer. He suspected gangs of Irish were being paid to stuff ballot boxes. In a rage, he called them "Wandering, roving, robbing, Irish. Robbing, bloated, pockmarked Catholic Irish." Herndon had to admit Lincoln himself did not feel that way about the Irish. Lincoln, he said, "had no prejudices against any class, . . . tolerating—as I never could—even the Irish."

Casual anti-Irish sentiment was rampant. Sullivan Ballou, a Union soldier whose celebrated letters to his wife Sarah formed a major centerpiece of the groundbreaking Ken Burns PBS history on the Civil War, was downright racist in a letter to Sarah that was quite different in tone to the warm and fuzzy love letters. Marching through Virginia on July 19,1861, he wrote, "We can get nothing from the people here, they are all against us. They all live miserably, I think, and the slaves are to me more filthy than our Irish."

The much beloved author of *Little Women*, Louisa May Alcott, was scathing about the "incapable" Irish and happily used a "No Irish Need Apply" addendum on her help-wanted ads.

Massachusetts was the hotbed of the Know-Nothings, the state where the most destitute Irish were landing. Not surprisingly, the Irish saw in them the mirror image of the landlords they had fled in Ireland after being driven off their land. Here now was a similar group trying to destroy them again.

Little wonder the Irish signed up for the Democratic Party in droves, seeking a job and a new start, which that party was offering to many off the boat.

Lincoln, in fact, correctly believed the slave issue to be of far more importance than ethnic strife, but the Irish, mindful of the rumors swirling around about his affinity for the Know-Nothings, kept their distance. It would take a civil war and inspired Irish leadership from Thomas Francis Meagher, Archbishop Hughes of New York, and others to bring them together.

It was not surprising, then, that Lincoln knew the Irish—he probably encountered more Irish personally than any other president, bar JFK. A million Irish had flooded in during the Famine years. In 1859, the entire population of the US was just twenty-three million, The Irish had a huge impact. Chicago, the nearest big city to Lincoln, had twenty percent of its population described as Irish. Springfield, home of his law office, too became an Irish hotbed.

John G. Nicolay and John Hay, Lincoln's biographers who served him in the White House, described Springfield as Lincoln found it when he moved there.

"The town was built on the edge of the woods, the north side touching the timber, the south encroaching on the prairie. . . . [T]here were, of course, no pavements, or sidewalks; an attempt at crossings was made by laying down large chunks of wood. The houses were almost all wooden, and were disposed in rectangular blocks."

A large square had been left in the middle of the town, in anticipation of future greatness, and when Lincoln began his residence, the work of clearing the ground for the new state house was already going forward. In one of the largest houses looking on the square, at the northwest corner, the county court had its offices, and other rooms in the building were let to lawyers. One of these was occupied by John Stuart, Lincoln's first law partner.

In Lincoln's hometown of Springfield the Irish were becoming an important group, especially at election time. Lincoln would have problems with that.

CHAPTER SIX

Lincoln Takes an Axe Handle to the Irish

The first Irish immigrants to Springfield began arriving in the 1830s and were middle-to-upper class, according to a master's thesis by Christopher Elliott Wallace that has been preserved in the Sangamon Valley Collection.

These early immigrants operated dry goods stores, inns, and sawmills. They were doctors, pharmacists, lawyers, and politicians. But the greatest influx of immigrants from Ireland came in the mid-1840s, after blight killed off the potato crop. This was a different kind of Irish—malnourished, poor, and desperate for a new life.

The Irish headed for the major US cities with dreams of starting all over in America and grabbing their own sliver of the American dream. Springfield, a boomtown developing and expanding quickly, seemed a natural halting place for the Irish. About 87,000 made their way to Illinois.

Illinois became a state in 1818. In the 1830s and 1840s, the Irish and Germans came from New York and Boston by way of the Erie Canal and the Great Lakes or on the new National Road. They settled the central and northern counties and looked to a bright future. The railroad arrived in 1852. When Lincoln left for the White

House in 1860, the population of Springfield was 10,000, about twenty percent of which were Irish.

But they were not welcome. The reception was cold, bordering on hatred. The established churches resented this new ethnicity and religion suddenly in their midst. "Intemperance, Sabbath-breaking and profanity all around," was one description of the unwashed Irish by a local preacher.

The Irish lived cheek by jowl in a decrepit series of buildings on the north side of town, known as "Chicken Row." Poverty bred bigotry and violence, and the Irish were often in the center of it. The Irish neighborhood was renamed "Battle Row."

For an ambitious Republican politician like Lincoln, the Irish represented a real difficulty. Springfield had closely-contested elections and rumors of traveling Irish being brought in to vote were widespread. Emigrant Irish stuffing the ballot boxes was a reality in New York; Lincoln did not want to see it in Springfield. In his 1858 senatorial election, Lincoln was convinced he could win if Irish ballot stuffing was avoided.

"I now have a high degree of confidence that we shall succeed if we are not overrun with fraudulent votes to a greater extent than usual." Lincoln claimed to have seen "Celtic gentlemen with their black carpet bags in their hands."

"What I most dread," he wrote, "is that they (the Democrats) will introduce into doubtful districts numbers of men who are legal voters in all respects save for residency. And will swear to residence and thus put it beyond our power to exclude him."

He was especially referring to Irish railroad workers being drafted in to vote. Lincoln suggested infiltrating such groups and exposing them at the right moment as unlawful.

He was not wrong to be fearful. In the 1858 election, Senator Stephen Douglas had the full support of the railroad barons for his approval of their expansionist plans. The workers were mainly Irish. Noted Civil War historian Allen C. Guelzo stated Lincoln feared railroad bosses "sending road gangs of Irish Catholics down the line, dropping them off in strategic districts days or weeks before the election to perform grading and repairs, and to turn up on Election Day to vote as though they were permanent residents."

Lincoln knew the Irish community in his Springfield were immigrants striving to start a new life. Unlike a lot of his contemporaries, Lincoln never viewed all immigrants as the same. However, he much preferred the Germans, who were fleeing a failed revolution and who were better educated than the Irish. One of his closest German allies, Gustave Koerner, was a pallbearer at his funeral.

The German community was led in many key positions by highly-educated German 48ers, revolutionaries who had fomented a democratic revolution in Germany in 1848 and fled to America after that. Intellectual, educated, and driven by visions of democratic freedoms, they were obvious fellow travelers for Lincoln. The scruffy Irish, fleeing famine and persecution, had no such hold on the future president.

Yet his wisdom in refusing to stereotype and blacken the Irish came though when all around him, including his wife and law partner, happily vilified them, and Lincoln was still perfectly capable of separating the political issues he disagreed with them on from his innate concern for all underdogs, which was such a measure of his life. Why else would his domestic staff both in Springfield and in the White House be composed of so many Irish immigrants?

His notoriously anti-Irish law partner, Herndon, aided and abetted the negative sentiments, saying the rumors of imported Irishmen voting was "no humbug cry" and asking, "What shall we do? Shall we tamely submit to the Irish, or shall we arise and cut their throats? If blood is shed in Illinois to maintain the purity of the ballot box and the rights of the popular will, do not be at all surprised."

A local newspaper, *The Jacksonville Sentinel*, took Lincoln to task for being anti-Irish. Though, in a strange context they accused him of being a "holy horror of all Irishmen and other adopted citizens who have sufficient self-respect to believe themselves superior to the Negro."

Herndon relates a specific event where Lincoln was prepared to use violence against the Irish.

"Once in Springfield, the Irish voters meditated taking possession of the polls. News came down the street that they would permit
nobody to vote but those of their own party.

"Mr. Lincoln seized an axe-handle from a hardware store and
went alone to open the way to the ballot box."

Lincoln was enormously strong, and his threat to fight was no
idle one.

In the 1858 election, Senator Douglas was re-elected to the Senate against Lincoln, but scholars agree the Irish vote was hardly the
main factor. Much more important was the power of the incum-
bency role, which meant Douglas had the railroad barons and scores
of favors and promises to dispense. He also had the Irish.

CHAPTER SEVEN

The Irish, Douglass, and Lincoln in the 1860 Election

Famine-tossed, starving, and homeless when they arrived, the Irish also faced incredible derision and hatred after they arrived on America's teeming shore. But there was no going back.

The hatred was palpable. An editorial in *The Chicago Tribune* in 1855 stated, "Who does not know that the most depraved, debased, worthless, and irredeemable drunkards and sots which curse the community are Irish Catholics?"

Even Theodore Roosevelt stated in the 1880s that "the average Catholic Irishman of the first generation, as represented in the [New York State] Assembly [is a] low, venal, corrupt, and unintelligent brute."

In *Harper's Weekly* a few years earlier, it was stated, "Irishmen . . . have so behaved themselves that nearly seventy-five percent of our criminals and paupers are Irish; that fully seventy-five percent of the crimes of violence committed among us are the work of Irishmen; that the system of universal suffrage in large cities has fallen into discredit through the incapacity of the Irish for self-government."

As Graydon Wilson, an Irish American expert noted, "In short, most Americans viewed Irish Catholics as people prone to violence, crime, corruption, drunkenness, and ignorance. They also viewed them as members of a church that was both wrong theologically and scheming to overthrow the American republic."

Even the sainted freed black slave Frederick Douglass found fault, blaming drunkenness, not the British, for the flight of millions from Ireland.

Douglass, who once wrote, "I have spent some of the happiest moments of my life since landing in this country," about his Irish visit, was likely reflecting his disappointment at the Irish American failure to heed Daniel O'Connell's rallying cry against slavery in his open letter to Irish America.

The great Liberator, the outstanding Irishman of his generation, some would argue of any generation, was fearless in his condemnation of slavery.

In his "Address from the People of Ireland to their Countrymen and Countrywomen in America," he made a spirited call to join the movement of William Garrison and Frederick Douglass, which was signed on to by 60,000 Irish.

"America is cursed by slavery!" it stated. "JOIN WITH THE ABOLITIONISTS EVERYWHERE! They are the only consistent advocates of liberty. . . . CLING BY THE ABOLITIONISTS."

Yet the Irish in America were deeply suspicious. They had seen the deep strain of anti-Irishness and the birth of the Know-Nothing movement stem from those very same abolitionists such as Wendell Phillips and Elijah Lovejoy, who were naked in their anti-Catholic bias. William Garrison hated Catholicism and often wrote of the pope as the "Whore of Babylon." Irish Catholics off the boat were always going to have difficulty supporting such men.

Historian Tom Chaffin notes that Douglass was in fact an Anglophile, grateful forever to Britain for banning slavery in 1833. Douglass was also ambivalent about Catholics, writing after watching a parade of Catholic seminarians in Rome that he was sad "that they are being trained to defend dogmas and superstitions contrary to the progress and enlightenment of the age."

He had remarkably little insight into why the Irish were suffering and what was causing it. In a famous letter to William Garrison concerning his four-month sojourn in Ireland, he wrote, "The immediate, and it may be the main cause of the extreme poverty and beggary in Ireland, is intemperance. This may be seen in the fact that most beggars drink whiskey. . . . Drunkenness is still rife in Ireland. The temperance cause has done much—is doing much—but there is much more to do, and, as yet, comparatively few to do it."

When a figure of such stature as Douglass had such mixed views on the Irish, it was hardly surprising that anti-Irish sentiment was cresting just at the time that Lincoln was taking to the national stage.

Lincoln himself, given his politics and the extreme views of men like his law partner Herndon, was remarkably affable about the Irish, even in private correspondence and conversation. But he could never match what Stephen Douglas, a Democrat, his chief opponent in 1858 for the senate and 1860 for the White House, provided to them—all-out support and attention at a time when they were reviled.

An important part of the Irish attraction to the Democratic Party was "The Little Giant," Senator Stephen Douglas, whose career and Lincoln's were forever entwined. They even sought the same woman, Mary Todd Lincoln, at one time.

Though born in Maine, Douglas had more of a natural-frontier, restless mindset. In 1833 he moved to Cleveland, then to Winchester, Illinois, where he worked as an itinerant schoolteacher before settling in Jacksonville, Illinois, where he was admitted to the bar. He wrote to his Vermont family, "I have become a Western man, have imbibed Western feelings, principles, and interests, and have selected Illinois as the favorite place of my adoption."

During his stellar political career, Douglas believed slavery should be decided by popular sovereignty, effectively leaving it to each state to decide its own position.

The Irish liked Douglas, given he was their Democratic Party candidate. He courted their votes at a time when they were widely shunned, and did not hesitate to use the race card with them.

Douglas told one nakedly racist story to illustrate the dangers of siding with Lincoln. In the story, freed slave Frederick Douglass was reputed to have come to an Illinois town in a fancy carriage. The Republican owner of the carriage was forced to ride on top of the vehicle while Douglass and the rich man's white wife and daughter rode inside.

"Black Republicans think that the Negro ought to be on a social equality with your wives and daughters, and ride in a carriage with your wife, while you drive the team," Stephen Douglas told his listeners. The message was clear: *"'Fred' Douglass wants your white wife and daughters."*

As historian Patrick Young noted, "The specter of white men having to turn their wives over to freed black men and being forced to serve the freed slave, as the black slave had once been forced to serve the white man, was the image of abolition served daily in the Democratic press to their newly arrived immigrant readers."

As his near-namesake Frederick Douglass noted, "The Irish people, warm-hearted, generous, and sympathizing with the oppressed everywhere, when they stand upon their own green island, are instantly taught, on arriving in this Christian country, to hate and despise the colored people.

"They are taught to believe that we eat the bread which of right belongs to them. The cruel lie is told the Irish, that our adversity is essential to their prosperity."

Stephen Douglas took his initial 1837 congressional campaign against Lincoln's law partner, John Stuart, into the Irish labor camps, where they were building the Michigan Canal project.

Whigs hooted that the Douglas idea of democracy meant having this diminutive figure (he was either five feet or five feet four, depending on reporting) addressing an Irish rabble about the importance of immigrants. Douglas was not above exaggeration either, saying he was Irish, descended from a long line of phantom McDouglasses. "I expect to get all the votes," he dryly told a friend.

He did, and lost by only thirty-seven votes to John Stuart, Lincoln's law partner, because of the Irish vote support. He learned to depend on them and deliver for them.

But most importantly, the Irish and other immigrant groups supported Douglas because the Whigs tried every available means to
disenfranchise them since they were recent immigrants and known
Democratic voters. The blacklisting of emigrants from voting effort
was especially promoted by Lincoln's then-party in Illinois.

Douglas fought tooth and nail to prevent that. He succeeded
with a brilliant lawyerly maneuver before the Illinois Supreme
Court, which saved the recent immigrant right to vote for at least
two elections.

In the process, the "Little Giant" developed even closer links
with the Irish. While he was not about to rally against the abolition
of slavery in new states, he was perfectly prepared to defend immigrants and their right to vote and did so in brilliant fashion. He also
visited them in their labor camps.

The Irish suffered dreadful conditions in those camps, as historian Allen Guelzo wrote. They were disease-ridden, and safety
standards were zero. Workers were only one injury away from complete destitution.

They were also vilified in Lincoln's Midwest. *The Chicago Tribune* wrote that the Scandinavians, Germans, French, English, and
Scotch would always "be counted on the side of free institutions."
The Irish, however, "have signally failed to comprehend the spirit of
freedom."

Protestant moralism mixed with Know-Nothing fervor on the
Republican/Whig side, making it inevitable that the Democratic
Party would provide the home for the Irish.

Douglas had also supported an Irish movement known as
"Young America," based on the radical Young Irelanders group
who sparked insurrection in Ireland. The American group optimisti-
cally called for the US to intervene militarily in Sicily and Ireland to
ensure their freedom. Douglas was all in.

He loved to tell stories about his Irish supporters and their
enthusiasm for him. On the campaign trail for his first race for congressman in Illinois in 1837, Douglas spoke at an Irish rally for him
in Joliet, Illinois, where hundreds of Irish worked on the canal. Most

were recent immigrants, well aware of the vilification of their kind. In Douglas they had a defender and hero.

Douglas said, "I had an appreciative audience; they cheered me; in fact they were too friendly. I was extolling the patriotic nature of Ireland, the virtues of her people, the bravery of her sons, and beauty of her daughters. I even referred to myself as being descended from a long line of patriotic sires of Irish descent. When I had said that a great big burly Irishman over six feet high rose and said, 'Do you say, Mr. Douglas, that you descended from the great McDouglasses of Ireland?' I said yes . . . Spreading out his brawny arms, he said, 'What a devil of a descent.'"

Douglas finished by stating he had the Irish vote in the bag.

He also mopped it up in his senate race against Lincoln. From 1850 to 1859, Douglas was the pre-eminent voice in the US senate but his relative moderation on the slavery issue opened a gap to his right for a Southern hardliner to exploit. Without that split Democratic vote, Douglas would very likely have won the White House.

Little wonder, then, that when 1860 rolled around and Lincoln faced off against Douglas, the Irish were solidly in the Douglas camp. As Tip O'Neill might have put it, "All politics is local." To his credit, Lincoln never took them to task over it and the relationship, once antagonistic and suspicious, was about to take on a much warmer glow forged by war.

CHAPTER EIGHT

Lincoln's Irish White House Circle

The election of 1860 was never close, with the pro-slavery vote badly split. Lincoln took 40 percent of the vote, with Douglas second at 30 percent. Douglas was the only candidate to win both a pro- and anti-slave state. He won the Irish Catholic vote overwhelmingly, both North and South. Many Irish organizations stood guard during his rallies; there is one description of Ancient Order of Hibernian members forming a protective phalanx around him.

As Douglas faded from history (he would die a year later), Abraham Lincoln emerged in his full pomp.

On his first day in the White House, accompanied by his outgoing predecessor James Buchanan (arguably the worst president in history), they arrived at 1600 Pennsylvania Avenue, where usually the only security was the elderly Irish doorman Edward McManus. Old Edward had served every president since either Jackson or Polk, depending on the historian.

McManus is described around this time as "the short, thin, smiling, humorous-looking elderly Irishman, the all-but-historic doorkeeper who has been so great a favorite through so many administrations."

"He is as well liked by his seventh president as he was even by General Taylor," wrote William Stoddard, one of Lincoln's private secretaries. Stoddard says, "There is no end of quiet fun in him as well as intelligence, and his other name is Fidelity. He is said to have been the only man in the White House to make President Lincoln laugh."

He was also deeply trusted. Lincoln's son Tad was what we would today call developmentally disabled. McManus was often entrusted with his care, and they became very close.

He was also the keeper of secrets. As Stoddard wrote, only McManus had any idea where Lincoln had headed when he took frequent solitary trips outside the White House.

It did not matter who was seeking him, cabinet secretary, congressman, or senator, McManus's answer was always the same.

"He's gone out, gentlemen. He didn't say where he was going, sir. If he's not at Mr. Seward's, it's most likely he has gone to some other place," was how Stoddard described this oft-repeated scene when Lincoln would set out by himself to find a general, a colleague, or a friend on a moment's impulse.

Stoddard stated McManus did not approve of some of Lincoln's antics, writing that "Old Edward" had "his own ideas of presidential dignity" and "did not approve of the fact that Mr. Lincoln had roped his own trunks and boxes in Springfield, and marked them, 'A. Lincoln, Washington, D.C.,' the night before starting on his trip to the capital. The President, no less!"

Old Edward was equally appalled when Mr. Lincoln went out to Pennsylvania Avenue: "Sure he was only waving his arm and shouting at a newsboy to bring him the morning paper. The President of the United States, no less!"

The elderly Irishman and fellow Gael Thomas Burns, who guarded the second floor, were it as regards internal security. As historian James Conroy notes, it was a kind of "Mutt and Jeff" arrangement. Lincoln was sure he was safe, believing assassinations were not in the American mindset.

The Irish connections Lincoln cultivated upset the blue-nosed clique.

Journalist Noah Brooks informed his readers in 1863 that "the President has succeeded in getting about him a corps of attaches of

Hibernian descent whose manner and style (were) as about as disagreeable as can be."

There was one exception, Brooks wrote. "Charlie, a valet whose services during our late visit to the Army of the Potomac I hold in grateful remembrance. That was Charles Forbes, who was present and a key figure at Ford's Theater on the night of the assassination."

Forbes was exceptionally close to the president, who called him Charlie. He accompanied him everywhere, including to the secret peace talks in February 1865 with Confederate leaders at Fort Monroe, when he and Charlie sneaked out of the White House to attend.

McManus, Burke, Forbes, Burns, O'Leary, Mangan, McGee, the list went on. Clearly Lincoln was comfortable with Irish around, even though many in his cabinet and party despised them.

He was not a hard taskmaster, but kept a distance. Secretary Stoddard wrote, "Towards his immediate subordinates, private secretaries, messengers, and other officials or servants, it may almost be said that he had no manner at all, he took their presence and the performance of their duties so utterly for granted. Not one of them was ever made to feel, unpleasantly, the fact of his inferior position by reason of any look or word of the President. All were well assured that they could not get a word from him unless the business which brought them to his elbow justified them in coming."

Even after battle defeats, Lincoln appeared to internalize the strain. Aides spoke of the heavy "tramp tramp" across the bedroom floor over their heads from the residential part of the White House after major defeats like Antietam and Fredericksburg. Back and forth until the early hours, Lincoln would go walking. They remembered his amazing resilience too, often appearing the next day with virtually no sleep ready to press on with the war.

There were certainly a lot of Irish at 1600 Pennsylvania Avenue; the building itself designed by an Irishman, architect James Hoban. Lincoln was also a huge fan of the writing of "Private Miles O'Reilly," a pseudonym for Irish emigrant Charles Halpine who had achieved officer status in the Union Army. Halpine wrote as Miles to critique those prosecuting the war and attack those leaders not devoted enough to Lincoln. Lincoln would sometimes wake one of his personal secretaries late at night and read gobs of O'Reilly to him as he battled his own insomnia.

It was hardly surprising there were so many Irish on the White House staff. Salaries were $800 a year when the average working man was making just $300 and jobs were highly sought after. Oftentimes, Irish were discriminated against when seeking such jobs, but not under Lincoln.

It is clear from one eyewitness account that Lincoln had no prejudice against the Irish. Laurance Mangan's brother was a White House coachman. Laurance recalled a week in which he substituted for his sick brother:

> President Lincoln was a grand man. Quiet and gentle in every respect, he was always thoughtful of those who served him, and although I was but a youngster in those days and not very long over (from) Ireland, Mr. Lincoln treated me with the same consideration he always bestowed on his regular men. President Lincoln was spending the summer at what is now the Soldiers' Home grounds, occupying the house of the governor of the Home as was then the custom, and it was there I reported to him. I drove him down to the offices that first morning and that evening when we returned, the President asked me to have the horses around again after supper, as he wanted to go out and look at the stars through that big new telescope they had installed at the naval observatory. I drove him out there that night and was also permitted to look through the telescope.
>
> The trip to the observatory was about the only long one on which I drove the President. It sounds funny, I know, to talk about that as a long trip this day and time but it was a fairly long distance in those days. Mr. Lincoln was very regular about his habits. He called for his carriage every morning about the same hour, and while I was with him at least, he left for his home every night about the same time. He was greatly

interested in his children and they used to come to meet him and ride up to the house with him.

The Old Soldiers' Home was located three miles from the White House on one of the highest points in the topography. Lincoln stayed in a thirty-four room Gothic cottage there and found the cooler breezes beneficial. He went there every June to November from 1862 to 1864 and wrote much of the Emancipation Proclamation there.

One-third of the residents of the main house were Irish soldiers who had fought for the Union and were disabled. Immigrants had little or no family structures to take care of them, so they fell back on institutional care. Despite the name of the institution, the average age was only forty-one; ten percent were under thirty years of age. The Old Soldiers' Home became the forerunner of the veterans' hospitals movement, where those who fought wars for their country were housed and helped with their lives after the combat stopped. Lincoln spent countless hours among them. He heard the Irish language used extensively and gathered a store of Irish stories. His opinion of the benefits of emigration after contact with the Irish and other foreign soldiers soared.

He wrote: "I regard our emigrants as one of the principal replenishing streams provided by Providence to repair the ravages of internal war and the waste of national strength and health."

Not all Irish employed by the White House were reputable, however.

Cornelius O'Leary was a doorkeeper to the president's office who replaced Edward McManus. McManus had been fired in the strangest of circumstances by Mrs. Lincoln. Given her own financial problems, it was strongly rumored by an opposition newspaper that she had done so to place O'Leary in the job, where he would solicit bribes for access to the president and share the rewards with her.

He was found to have been taking bribes of up to $50 in order to expedite the freedom of Confederate prisoners who could take an amnesty oath not to fight again against the Union.

Contemporary journalist Noah Brooks recorded what happened:

Everybody knows that it is the constant practice of the
President to discharge prisoners of war who take the amnesty
oath upon proper application being made by the Congressmen
who represent the districts where their homes are located.
This application was made by a Union Congressman from
Kentucky, and, it now appears, was laid before the President
by H.W. Harrington, of Indiana, into whose hands O'Leary
gave the paper.

The same result would have been attained if the application had been sent to the President through the hands of his
Private Secretary, but Etheridge (Emerson Etheridge, a congressman from Tennessee who somehow became involved),
with his innate love of intrigue, appeared to prefer bribing a
servant to accomplish what any man could do in the regular
way, and then, having extorted forcibly his bribe from the
tempted servant, he rushed his own disgrace and shame into
print, as if he had done a very fine thing.

O'Leary, of course, was instantly dismissed from service
when the president ascertained what had been done; but whatever may be the public verdict in his case no sane man can
regard with any degree of tolerance the part which Emerson
Etheridge has played in the matter.

O'Leary himself was an extraordinary figure and may well have
been scapegoated to protect Mrs. Lincoln, who may have inveigled
him into the scheme.

O'Leary was an adventurer who left Tipperary at an early age.

In 1858, he was part of the Irish Papal Brigade, charged with
restoring the pope to Rome after the Garibaldi rebellion. He then
came to the US and fought in the Civil War, enlisting in the Irish Brigade. He was wounded at Malvern Hill.

On his recovery, he was appointed postmaster of Lincoln Hospital in D.C. Then he replaced the legendary McManus as the

White House doorkeeper and found himself in hot water over the pardons scheme after Lincoln himself personally looked into the issue.

O'Leary was a Fenian and was asked to go back and help organize units for the abortive rebellion that happened in 1867. En route, he was captured and jailed by the British but was later released on the understanding that he would return to America. He did and resettled in Brooklyn, and he still has direct descendants in the New York area.

But the Lincolns had not heard the last of "Old Edward." After Mrs. Lincoln fired McManus, according to historian Stephen B. Oates, "she and Lincoln had an ugly scene. In her misery, Mary told one of her male friends about the quarrel, but later wrote the man to keep it a 'sacredly guarded' secret that she'd talked with him about her marital troubles. Because she knew how Lincoln grieved 'over any coolness of mine,' she went to him, and they made up and had 'quite a little laugh together.'"

McManus did not go quietly. He moved to New York, where he told stories about financial improprieties by Mrs. Lincoln and some say even alleged affairs. One of his key listeners was the influential newspaper editor Thurlow Weed, who widely publicized the allegations, which impacted Mrs. Lincoln's historical reputation.

Mary Todd Lincoln was furious. She wrote to a New York acquaintance that she could scarcely believe that people were taking McManus's allegations seriously. She described him as a "discarded menial" and suggested he was out of his mind. Clearly McManus knew too much for her liking.

Mary Todd Lincoln never did share her husband's fondness for the Irish, dating back to her treatment of her Irish servant girls. She treated the venerable McManus no better. She always preferred the company of Elizabeth Keckley, a former slave. Perhaps she felt more at home, as her family had been slave owners.

Her temper and frequent demands, however, led even Lincoln's loyal secretary John Hay to call her "The Hellcat." Once, when Lincoln was reviewing the Army of the Potomac, Mary arrived late and found Major General O. C. Ord's wife riding alongside the president.

In a jealous rage, she gave the unfortunate woman a tongue-lashing that reduced her to tears, and she berated Lincoln in front of his officers. This incident and others led Julia Grant, wife of Lieutenant General Ulysses S. Grant, to declare she would not spend another evening with "that woman."

CHAPTER NINE

Lincoln's Love
for Irish Ballads Displayed

The White House Historical Association (WHA) notes that despite having no musical talent, Lincoln used music as a panacea for getting away from his problems and relaxing. Among his favorites, the WHA says, were the Irish ballads "Kathleen Mavourneen," "Last Rose of Summer," "Old Rosin the Beau," and "Annie Laurie," all of which held their own special poignancy and charm.

Of all the songs of the Civil War that evoke that period, "Kathleen Mavourneen," an Irish ballad of love and farewell, was a huge staple. Some believe that next to "Dixie," it was the most popular song, especially on the Confederate side.

That is not surprising, as it was written by Englishman Frederick Crouch, who came to America in 1849 and joined the Confederate army as a trumpeter. Despite its origins, Irish emigrant soldiers adopted it as their own.

On Crouch's death in 1896, it was estimated that two million copies of the song sheet music had been sold, but he had failed to copyright it and got little or no money as a result.

The song, which means "Kathleen My Beloved" is a sad song of emigration and departure. It exploded in popularity after Irish soprano Catherine Hayes sang the song for Queen Victoria in 1849. Hayes, on tour, sang it across the United States and, as a result, "Kathleen Mavourneen" became a staple.

Writer James Parton recalled opera singer Adelaide Phillips performing it in a posh home in New York and a young Irish maid sobbing.

It became a historic part of the Civil War era after Almira Hancock, wife of Union hero General Winfield Hancock, recalled it was sung at an emotional farewell dinner for a group of army officers and colleagues just before the Civil War began.

Wes Clark, a Civil War buff, noted, "It was in the early summer of 1861 that the famous farewell party noted in Almira Hancock's memoirs was held at the Hancock home in Los Angeles. Close friends like Albert Sidney Johnston, Richard Garnett, and Lewis Armistead bid their final goodbyes to the Hancocks. Johnston would be killed at Shiloh, and Garnett and Armistead would later battle Hancock's forces at Gettysburg."

Will Gorenfeld, also a Civil War buff, states, "Winfield Scott Hancock, Lewis Armistead, and Dick Garnett had all served together in California and Mexico in the 6th US Infantry. They were close friends. Armistead and Garnett died during Pickett's futile charge against General Hancock's position. General Johnston died at Shiloh."

The story of the grand party first appeared in Almira Hancock's biography of her late husband, which was published in 1887, a year after the general's death. Given the source, several generations of historians have taken it on faith that there was a grand farewell party at the Hancock's Los Angeles home in which six or so future Confederate officers, including Albert Sidney Johnston, Garnett, and Armistead, all attended. Mrs. Hancock wrote about the sadness of the evening as Mrs. Johnston sang "Kathleen Mavourneen." At this, she said, "Hearts were filled with sadness over the surrendering of life-long ties."

Some historians have since questioned that account, but the

song has become enshrined in Civil War folklore with its opening verse, known to hundreds of thousands:

Kathleen, Mavourneen, the grey dawn is breaking,
The horn of the hunter is heard on the hill;
The lark from her light wing the bright dew is shaking;
Kathleen, Mavourneen, What! slumbering still?
Oh! hast thou forgotten how soon we must sever?
Oh! hast thou forgotten, this day we must part;
It may be for years, and it may be forever?
Oh! why art thou silent, thou voice of my heart?
It may be for years, and it may be forever?
Oh! why art thou silent, Kathleen, Mavourneen?

In 1862, soon after the death of their beloved twelve-year-old son Willie, the Lincolns invited Adelina Patti, the most famous singer of her time, for a recital. Her second-to-last song that night in the Red Room was by Irish composer Thomas Moore, entitled "The Last Rose of Summer." It was a Lincoln favorite, and one of ten songs on Mary Todd Lincoln's music box, which is now in the Abraham Lincoln Presidential Library and Museum in Springfield, Illinois.

As a much older woman, Patti recorded "The Last Rose of Summer" on a phonograph in 1905, readily available on YouTube. Thus, you can hear the very same voice and song the Lincolns listened to all those years ago—a bridge back in time to what Lincoln heard.

CHAPTER TEN

Two Irish Become the First Casualties of the Civil War

Following the 1860 election of Lincoln, the decision by seven southern states to secede made the Civil War inevitable. In Charleston, South Carolina, the Confederacy demanded the removal of the Union army there, but the Union commander, Major Robert Anderson, prepared for a lengthy siege by barricading his men in the sea fort known as Fort Sumter.

Repeated demands by Confederates that the Yankees yield the fort were refused by Major Anderson. Beginning at close to dawn, at 4:30 a.m. on April 12, 1861, the Rebels commenced firing. After a day and a half, the Union garrison agreed to evacuate. During the surrender ceremony a jammed cannon exploded, killing two Union soldiers on April 14.

Thus the first casualties of the American Civil War were two Irishmen, the first named as Private Daniel Hough from Tipperary, who was thirty-six-years old. The second soldier killed was Private Ed Galloway, an emigrant from Skibbereen, County Cork.

A few months later, Ed's brother Andrew was also killed. *The Cork Examiner* newspaper in Ireland carried Andrew's obituary on April 11, 1863:

At Baton Rouge, La., U.S.A. America, Major Andrew Galloway, son of the late John Galloway, Esq., Skibbereen. Having been wounded at the taking of Port Hudson, he was removed to Baton Rouge, where he died on the 9th July, a Christian soldier, fortified by all the rites of the Catholic Church, in the 26th year of his age.

His brother Edward was the first victim whose life was sacrificed in the present American war. He was killed at Fort Sumter, on the 13th April, 1861, aged 20 years.—May they rest in peace.

Daniel Hough was born in 1825 in Tipperary, Ireland. Irish historian Damian Shiels believes that based on a letter from Hough, or Howe's brother (there were different spellings of the name in official records), he was from the town of Nenagh. He emigrated to the US and enlisted in the US Army in October 1849. He remained in the army and was at Fort Sumter in April 1861 at the beginning of the Civil War.

He was one of the Union army defending Fort Sumter when the Confederates began attacking. An official account of his career states that he was an Irish immigrant who had enlisted in Battery D of the 1st United States Artillery Regiment.

After serving out his enlistment, he re-enlisted on December 6, 1859 at Ft. Moultrie, South Carolina. This time he was assigned to Battery E, 1st United States Artillery. His military record states that he had gray hair, blue eyes, a fair complexion, and was five feet eight inches tall.

Private Hough was serving as an artillerist, posted at Ft. Sumter, out in Charleston Harbor, when the Civil War began on the morning of April 12, 1861. The garrison put up a spirited defense, and the bombardment lasted until April 14, when the fort's commander, Major Robert Anderson, decided to surrender. The Confederates lobbed cannonballs heated in furnaces into the interior of the fort.

"They were coming down through the roofs of the barracks buildings and set those buildings on fire," a witness said.

The Union army was offered an honorable surrender and to give a 100-gun salute to the fallen fort.

A cannon fired prematurely on the 47th round, killing Union Pvt. Hough, the immigrant from Tipperary, Ireland—the first death of the Civil War.

Major General Abner Doubleday witnessed what occurred that April 14, 1861 when Hough died. "It happened that some flakes of fire had entered the muzzle of one of the guns after it was sponged. Of course, when the gunner attempted to ram the cartridge down it exploded prematurely, killing Private Daniel Hough instantly, and setting fire to a pile of cartridges underneath, which also exploded, seriously wounding five men. Fifty guns were fired in the salute."

In Washington, Lincoln had attended church services praying for a peaceful outcome to the Fort Sumter crisis. The death of the Irishmen in the Union blue uniforms helped convince him there was now no way back.

On April 15, 1861, President Abraham Lincoln called up 75,000 federal militia members and the Civil War began. By the time it was over 600,000 would be dead on the battlefields. It was a war like no other. Mary Todd Lincoln's brothers fought for the Confederacy. Stonewall Jackson's sister cut off all contact with him when he sided with the rebels. It was too often brother against brother, neighbor against neighbor, friends who were now foes. It would change America, and the world, forever.

Would the Irish who were flooding into the country go to war for Lincoln, whose Know-Nothing supporters they despised? The answer would soon become apparent.

CHAPTER ELEVEN

Three Men Convince the Irish to Fight for Lincoln: Thomas Francis Meagher

Three men forged the path for 150,000 Irishmen to fight and very likely save the Union. They were Thomas Francis Meagher, Archbishop John Hughes, and Michael Corcoran.

Another Irishman, General Philip Sheridan, arguably was the hammer on the anvil that brought the war to an end.

"In (Meagher) we see the entire arc of so much crucial Irish-American history in one man's life—persecution, famine, banishment, exile, revival, and finding your place in a strange land," Timothy Egan, author of *The Immortal Irishman*, a book about Meagher, says.

Thomas Francis Meagher was born in Waterford in 1823 and became the great hero of Irish America. He was the son of a prominent Catholic businessman who was an elected MP to the British Parliament from Waterford.

Meagher rejected his wealthy background and became a revolutionary. He was a key figure in the Young Irelanders, young men and some women who were tired of waiting in the shadow of Daniel O'Connell, the Liberator who they believed had failed to capitalize on the mass movement he had created. The Young Irelanders consisted of highly educated and committed young men, including Thomas Davis, who wrote "A Nation Once Again" and was the most prominent leader and polemicist in "The Nation" newspaper he founded.

The Young Irelanders built on the vision of Irish revolutionary Theobald Wolfe Tone who masterminded the 1798 Rising which hoped to achieve the unity of Catholic, Protestant, and dissenter, but did not shirk the staging of a violent revolution to bring it about.

This was the group Meagher was deeply drawn to. A speech in Dublin on July 28, 1846, was his defining moment. A young upstart committed to revolution, he went head-to-head with the O'Connell family, whose patriarch was the great Daniel O'Connell. O'Connell saw constitutional means as the way forward.

It was the same argument that had riven Ireland for centuries, even up to the present day. But young Meagher won this round heartily. Meagher turned on those who advocated no violence by recalling the American Revolution: "Abhor the sword, stigmatize the sword? No, my lord, for at its blow, a giant nation started from the waters of the Atlantic, and by its redeeming magic, and in the quivering of its crimson light, the crippled colony sprang into the attitude of a proud Republic—prosperous, limitless, and invincible!"

"It was thrilling music," said his friend and fellow compatriot Charles Gavan Duffy, editor of *The Nation*, "to wake the Irish from their national coma."

Two years later, and the young Demosthenes was on his way to penal servitude in Australia after the abortive 1848 Rising in Ireland. He was transported to a penal colony in Australia, from which he made a spectacular escape to America.

That escape was an incredible one. His father had paid for a boat to pick him up at a particular postage stamp-sized island off of Tasmania in a particular time frame. Loosely guarded, he fled the mainland of Tasmania for Waterhouse Island, located on a shipping channel linking the Indian Ocean to the Pacific. The journey to the island through shark-infested waters and foul weather nearly killed him, and he was dropped off on the tiny dot of an island only a square mile in size.

After ten days on Waterhouse Island and living off birds' eggs and fruit, a ship hove into view as arranged. *The Elizabeth Thomson,* organized in New York and paid for in Ireland by his father, had sailed the high seas and somehow found him within the expected time period—and at the correct location. Soon the ship was on the wide Pacific and New York bound.

The boat took him to Pernambuco, Brazil. From there, concealing himself in the last bag of sugar beneath deck on *The Acorn.* Meagher came to the United States. Arriving on May 27, 1852, he stepped off *The Acorn* into New York Harbor, a free man.

He was a sensation among Irish Americans when he arrived in New York, a genuine Irish hero who had spent his life fighting for Irish freedom. Here was the leader the Irish had been waiting for. As Timothy Egan reports in *Immortal Irishman*, his superb biography of Meagher, a Young Irelander supporter, Michael Cavanagh, was electrified to find Meagher in his midst.

"Frank and free, he was Tom Meagher—the best beloved of his race and generation...on him were centered the hopes of his exiled countrymen...to unite them for the attainment of Irish freedom."

The New York Times would have plenty to say about Meagher in the future. So would Abe Lincoln, who became a close friend, and so would Meagher himself, who was faithful to the last to the president he so dearly admired and placed the young Irish men of New York firmly on his side.

The New York Times remarked, "His arrival has created universal satisfaction here."

On his second night in town, dining at a friend's house, 7,000 Irish, including members of the famed all-Irish New York Fighting 69th unit, showed up outside with the Brooklyn Cornet Band. There was bedlam at his arrival. "Meagher in America!" proclaimed *The Nation* newspaper headline.

Meagher addressed huge public meetings, always on the topic of Irish freedom, but when the Civil War was imminent, he married the Irish thirst for freedom with the opportunity their new land had given them to start afresh. He was one of the key movers behind the Irish Brigade, a number of regiments that recruited Irish from across state lines, which was highly unusual at the time. The regiments coalesced under the names of the Irish Brigade and The Fighting 69th.

He called on the Irish to join en masse. "It is the duty of every freedom-loving citizen to prevent such a calamity (secession) at all hazards. Above all, it is the duty of us Irish citizens who aspire to establish a similar form of government in our native land."

On August 30, 1861, the brigade was officially created.

WAR DEPARTMENT, WASHINGTON.
August 30, 1861
COLONEL THOMAS F. MEAGHER, New York
SIR – The Regiment of infantry known as the Sixty-Ninth Infantry, which you offer, is accepted for three years, or during the war, provided you have it ready for marching orders in thirty days. This acceptance is with the distinct understanding that this department will revoke the commissions of all officers who may be found incompetent for the proper discharge of their duties.
Your men will be mustered into the United States service in accordance with General Orders Nos. 58 and 61.
You are further authorized to arrange with the colonels commanding of four other regiments to be raised to form a brigade, the brigadier-general for which will be designated hereafter by the proper authority of Government.
Very respectfully your obedient servant,
THOMAS A. SCOTT
Assistant Secretary of War.

For Lincoln, the Irish Brigade made certain sense, marrying a great fighting unit with Democratic supporters, which was quite a coup for the Republican president. He saw in Meagher the perfect foil for this strategy. His dealings with the Irish Brigade always reflected favorably on them, and he clearly admired Meagher.

On a visit to the Irish Brigade he made his sentiments clear that he wanted fair treatment for the brigade.

Executive Mansion
Major Gen. Halleck Feb. 12. 1863.
Gen. Meagher, now with me, says the Irish Brigade has had no promotion; and that Col. Robert Nugent & Col. Patrick Kelly, both of that Brigade have fairly earned promotion. They both hold commissions as Captains in the regular army. Please examine their records with reference to the question of promoting one or both of them.
Yours truly,
A. LINCOLN

Gen. T. Francis Meagher Washington, D.C.,
New York. June 16, 1863
Your dispatch received. Shall be very glad for you to raise 3,000 Irish troops, if done by the consent of, and in concert with, Governor Seymour.
A. LINCOLN

Major General Meade Executive Mansion,
Army of the Potomac Washington, April 9. 1864.
Suspend execution of private William Collins, Co. B. 69th. N.Y. Vols. Irish Brigade, and class him with other suspended cases.
A. LINCOLN

Lincoln also visited the Fighting 69th once and noted their bravery, grasping their banner and stating, "God bless the Irish."

The Fighting 69th Historian recorded that amazing visit by Lincoln to the regiment:

During Lincoln's visit to the army (after the battle of Malvern

Hill), 1st Lt. James M Birmingham, adjutant of the 88th New York, emerged from a swim in the river. With his wet underwear drying on his body, the Lieutenant walked over to the 69th camp to visit his brother.

When Birmingham turned a corner, he saw the president and Generals McClellan and Sumner speaking with Colonel Nugent. He ducked behind some cover and eavesdropped on the conversation. Forever after, the 88th's adjutant would remember that he saw Lincoln, impressed by the Irish Brigade's sacrifices, lift a corner of the 69th's flag 'and kiss it, exclaiming, 'God bless the Irish flag.'

Those were words that no British leader would ever speak, and Meagher recognized that. Lincoln had also called for freedom for Ireland when in Congress.

With Senator Stephen Douglas vanquished (he died in 1861), it was clear the Irish needed a new American political leader. Why not the president? Besides, were not the British rooting for a Confederate victory? What better way to prepare someday to do battle than sign up with the Union army?

Lincoln was a different kind of Republican, they argued. He had rejected the Know-Nothings, the anti-Catholic party. To the Irish, the Republican Party stood for two things: anti-Catholic and anti-slavery, and the former was far more important to them than the latter. Lincoln was different, however.

In her thesis on Thomas Francis Meagher, Montana scholar Angela Faye Thompson notes: "In *The Origins of the Republican Party*, William E. Gienapp summarized the (Republican) party's stance this way: 'The Republican Party projected an anti-Catholic image, a fact readily perceived by nativists and Catholic voters alike. The Republican Party decided to focus on two issues: anti-Slavery and anti-Catholicism. These two issues spelled success in the 1850s.'"

They were also at complete odds with each other. Why would the Irish fight for an alleged anti-Irish president? Most of the Irish

American press was adamantly opposed to Lincoln throughout the war.

Meagher persuaded many of them. He threw his influence behind Lincoln and became an outspoken opponent of slavery at a time when the majority of Irish in New York did not want to fight and die to free African slaves. He went further, demanding they be granted full citizenship, not just freedom. "The Black heroes of the Union army have not only entitled themselves to liberty but to citizenship," he declared.

He was fearless in his commitment to causes involving injustice anywhere and in his beloved Ireland.

Meagher received his general's commission directly from President Lincoln. "Lincoln liked Meagher, and vice versa," says Meagher biographer Timothy Egan, "even though they were in different political parties. Lincoln made time to see Meagher even when he saw no one else. Lincoln shrewdly named Meagher a general as a way to win over the Irish masses to the Union cause."

Like Lincoln, Meagher soft-pedaled the issue of slavery at first as the reason to go to war, before later coming out in full-throated support of emancipation.

When explaining his decision to back the Union side when so many joined or supported the Rebels, Meagher stated, "Duty and patriotism prompt me."

He said:

The Republic, that gave us an asylum—that is the mainstay of human freedom the world over—is threatened with disruption. It is the duty of every liberty-loving citizen to prevent such a calamity at all hazards. Above all is it the duty of us Irish citizens, who aspire to establish a similar form of government in our native land. It is not only our duty to America, but also to Ireland. We could not hope to succeed in our effort to make Ireland a Republic without the moral and material aid of the liberty-loving citizens of these United States.

English support for the Confederacy was a further spur to Irish enlistment. King Cotton, enabled by the slave trade, kept the English economy booming and led to a decided Confederate tilt.

Some ordinary English felt differently. Workers in a cotton mill in Lancashire refused to accept cotton from America picked by slaves. Lincoln wrote and praised them, saying it was "sublime Christian heroism, which has not been surpassed in any age or in any country."

The French Comte de Paris visited the US and wrote that the Irish "looked upon the war...as a favorable opportunity for preparing to crush England."

Shortly following his enlistment in the Fighting 69th New York, Meagher delivered one of his most influential speeches, "The Irish Soldier: His History and Present Duty to the American Republic."

Meagher stated that he remained a Democrat and a Union man. He said that although he had not voted for Lincoln, he was the legitimate president and the Confederate state was thus illegal:

> In a word, we find that there is not one substantial reason or pretext for this revolution. . . . How unnatural this war! How infamous! How horrible! But who began it?
>
> Hence it is that I have appeared in arms for the National Government; and hence it is that I have already and do invoke my countrymen to take up arms in the same righteous cause.
>
> I will not remind them that when driven from their own land, when their huts were pulled down or burned above their heads. . . . Irishmen came here and had a new life infused into them, a fertile soil beneath their feet. . . . I will not remind my countrymen of the sympathy and substantial aid, which the people of America have given them. . . . This is the only country where the Irish people can reconstruct themselves and become a power.

His speech closed with a mighty call to arms.

> Then up, Irishmen! Up! Take the sword in hand! Down to the

banks of the Potomac! Let those who can, do so; and I believe I speak consistently with the views of your esteemed Chief Magistrate, when I say that every facility will be accorded those Irishmen who wish to enlist under the banner of the State; and I have no doubt that, somehow or other indeed with every facility—the Irishmen regimented together, carrying the green flag with the Stars and Stripes and the State arms, will one day find themselves in the Irish Brigade. . . .

Meagher acknowledged his own opposition to Lincoln's election, but said he respected the democratic process. "I care not to what party the [president] has belonged. I care not upon what . . . platform he may have been elected. The platform disappears before the Constitution."

Respect for the constitutional office of the presidency trumped partisan political consideration, he told his audiences. The Southerner, he said, "substitutes for the rule of the ballot box . . . the rule of the bayonet . . . against the will of the majority of the people."

Meagher acknowledged that some of the same men who sought to exclude the Irish were now in Lincoln's government. In a speech in Boston after an anti-Irish riot, Meagher spoke of a new era for Irish Americans: "I proclaim . . . Know-Nothingism is dead. This war . . . brought with it this result, that the Irish soldier will henceforth take his stand proudly by the side of the native-born and will . . . look him straight and sternly in the face and tell him that he has been equal to him in his allegiance to the Constitution."

He was adamant that by signing for the Union, immigrants were proving the Know-Nothings wrong.

He was steadfast for Lincoln, even when he fired General George McClellan, a commander beloved by the Irish troops. "Commanding brigade composed principally of Irish soldiers, the Brigadier General considers it not out of place to remind them that the great error of the Irish people in their struggle for an independent national existence has been their passionate and blind adherence to an individual instead of to a country and cause." He warned that a Southern victory would "encourage the designs of kings and queens and knaves to whom this great commonwealth . . . has been . . . a source of envy."

Meagher's hold on the Irish American community was such that Lincoln's decision to appoint Meagher as commanding officer of the Irish Brigade was a turning point for recruitment.

Some enlisted men were huge Lincoln admirers, as demonstrated by the following story unearthed by ace historian Damian Shiels from the archives of *The Irish American* newspaper in September 1861.

A few nights ago, we had a birth in the 37th, the wife of Private Dooley, of Co. K, bringing him an heir, which the officers forthwith adopted as their protégé, to be the future 'child of the regiment.' He was baptized on Sunday, the 15th, by Father Tissot, Col. Burke, and Mrs. Lieutenant Barry standing sponsors in behalf of the regiment.

As soon as pay-day comes, it is proposed to contribute a handsome sum, which is to be deposited in bank there to accumulate to the credit of the child when he comes of age. Already has been received several presents of clothing, from kind ladies in Washington and the President is expected to contribute his mite, also, towards his namesake, Abraham Lincoln Dooley."

Such happy occasions aside, still the old ways died hard. William Tecumseh Sherman, whose march to the sea in 1864 would bring the South to its knees, viewed the Irish Brigade at Fort Corcoran and remarked, "No cohesion, no real discipline, no respect for authority." Sherman, born a Presbyterian was re-baptized as a Catholic and had as a son a Catholic priest. Nonetheless he clearly disliked the Irish and treated Meagher's men like "farm animals, with a stench to go with them," Meagher's biographer Timothy Egan states.

That was surprising, given that Sherman's beloved son Willie attended Notre Dame and another son, Charlie, whom he never knew, died at age ten months and was buried at Notre Dame.

The level of anti-Irish Catholic sentiment at the top of the Union army has been debated. The Know-Nothing Party, though fading out, certainly had followers. General Ulysses S. Grant, of Irish heritage through his grandmother Simpson (his great-grandfather had left Dungannon, County Tyrone, in the 1730s), admitted in his memoirs he had joined the Know-Nothings for a brief period.

Grant wrote about his political leanings in his memoir. "Most of my neighbors had known me as an officer of the army with Whig proclivities. They had been on the same side, and, on the death of their party, many had become Know-Nothings, or members of the American Party. There was a lodge near my new home, and I was invited to join it. I accepted the invitation; was initiated; attended a meeting just one week later, and never went to another afterwards.

"I have no apologies to make for having been one week a member of the American Party for I still think native-born citizens of the United States should have as much protection, as many privileges in their native country, as those who voluntarily select it for a home."

Grant was the first US president to visit Ireland, albeit while out of office, in 1879.

It was not all smooth sailing. The anti-Catholic label stuck to Grant in Ireland. Catholic members of the Cork City Town Council objected to Grant's visit. A member of the council, a Mr. Barry, said the ex-President had "got up the no popery cry" in America. Several others agreed, and there was no dissenting voice. General Grant was disinvited to Cork.

The New York Herald dryly noted, "The Town Council of Cork seems to be better Catholics than the pope himself." They pointed out that his two closest friends in the Union army, General William Tecumseh Sherman and General Phil Sheridan, were both Catholics and vouched for his lack of anti-Catholic sentiment. But nothing would sway the Cork Town Council, so Grant went to Ulster instead.

It has been suggested that the reason General George Meade had difficulty getting promoted, until his heroics as commander at

Gettysburg, was because of an Irish Catholic branch of his ancestry and the influence of Know-Nothings within the army.

The Irish were still held in contempt in high places. Leading New York lawyer George Templeton Strong wrote privately that the Irish were "creatures that crawl and eat dirt and poison every county they infest."

They sometimes saw their attempts to enlist blocked by bigotry. For example, the quartermaster general of Wisconsin turned away Irish recruits. "There are enough young Americans to put down this trouble inside of ninety days," he said, "and we do not want any red-faced foreigners." By the end of the war, the red-faced foreigners would have played a key role in saving the Union that so many had sought to remove them from.

As historian Terry L. Jones has pointed out: "The Irish Brigade suffered the third-highest number of battlefield casualties of any Union brigade. Of the 7,715 men who served in its ranks, 961 were killed or mortally wounded, and approximately 3,000 were wounded. The number of casualties was more men than ever served in its ranks at any one time."

Some suspected they were being used as cannon fodder, so often were they in the front ranks and holding the hardest ground. It was a feeling widely believed by, among others, Archbishop John Hughes of New York. Time and again, at Bull Run, Antietam, and especially Fredericksburg, the Irish had been pushed into the vanguard and lost men in huge numbers. Only the Iron Brigade, today's marine equivalent, lost more by some accounts.

Craig Warren, a professor at Penn State Erie, spoke to the Virginia Humanities Council program "Backstory" about the blatant disregard by generals for Irish lives, especially by General Ambrose Burnside at Fredericksburg. He believes it played a role in the dreadful draft riot in New York City.

"Many Irish Americans decided that what had happened was that the Irish Brigade had been wantonly sacrificed during the battle by generals who saw them simply as cannon fodder. The war effort wasn't bringing people around to see the Irish as true

Americans, and so they turned their backs on that war effort and decided that it was not worth investing further time, energy, lives, and money into. It's not too much to say that you can draw a straight line between the Battle of Fredericksburg and the New York City draft riots of 1863."

In regards to Fredericksburg, *The London Times* correspondent William H. Russell (himself Irish-born) wrote, "Never at Fontenoy, Albuera, or at Waterloo was more undaunted courage displayed by the sons of Erin than during those six frantic dashes which they directed against the almost impregnable positions of their foe."

Despite the horrific losses throughout the campaign, Meagher never stopped trying to build up his Irish ranks. On February 12, 1863, on Lincoln's fifty-fourth birthday, Meagher met with President Lincoln, who looked terrible, the relentless onslaught of war and personal tragedy taking its toll. Meagher's courage and stance for the Union made him an important figure.

Lincoln listened silently, and Meagher made his pitch for a revived Irish brigade and more manpower, as well as overdue promotions. Lincoln heard him out, then wrote a letter seeking exactly what Meagher had asked for.

That November they met again. The president rose from his sickbed, and Meagher was the only visitor he saw that day. They talked about a new post for Meagher, perhaps with his new commander General Grant, which never came through. But Meagher had proven his usefulness, a fact readily acknowledged by Lincoln.

It was one of at least three meetings. Lincoln knew what he owed to the Irish and their bravery. After the First Battle of Bull Run, Lincoln came by the Irish Brigade and was greeted with lusty cheers. Meagher, still fuming over how Sherman had treated him and his Irish brigade, stepped forward when Lincoln asked if there was anything he could do for the Irish.

"Mr. President, I have cause for a grievance."

"Yes."

"This morning I went to Colonel Sherman, and he threatened to shoot me."

Lincoln, not wishing to get embroiled in a fight between officers joked, "If I were you and he threatened to shoot me I'd believe him." For once Meagher was speechless.

Meagher died in July 1867 under mysterious circumstances in Montana, where he had gone as territorial governor. He fell or was pushed off a ship. He had made many enemies, especially among radical Republicans and a group of self-styled vigilantes who hung or shot people they wanted rid of with impunity. His body was never found. Outside the state house in Montana stands a magnificent statue of him.

In one of his last letters to a friend he stated:

"I want my countrymen to place me up and beyond the sneers of these 'blackguards' who are ever so ready to run down an Irishman, whenever and wherever they have a chance."

At Meagher's funeral Mass in New York City, his eulogist Richard Gorman said, "Never forget this: he gave all, lost all for the land of his birth. He risked all for the land of his adoption, was her true and loyal soldier, and in the end died in her service. Would that his grave were on some Irish hillside, with the green turf above him."

Meagher sent the Irish to war more than anyone. They fought well. One hundred forty-six Irishmen were awarded the Medal of Honor, the highest by far of any immigrant group. They fought and many died for Lincoln and the Union.

The fight between the states and between Confederate Irish and Union Irish was beautifully summed up by Fighting 69th historian Claire Morris. During the siege of Petersburg "a truce was declared on the picket line and both sides mingled freely, exchanging newspapers, coffee, tobacco, and whiskey. The Northern and Southern Irishmen argued about the war when they had a chance.

"'A fine bunch of Irishmen you are, coming into the South and burning our farms and acting worse than the English ever did in Ireland,' said one of Mahone's Irish immigrant Confederates after he had been captured by a group of soldiers from the 69th New York.

"'Ah, hold yer whisht,' replied one of the New York Irishmen, 'A fine bunch of Irishmen you are, trying to break up the Union that gave ye a home and fighting for the rich slave owner.'"

There was surely very little answer for that.

CHAPTER TWELVE

Fighting for Lincoln:
the Irish Archbishop

The second Irishman who delivered the Irish into the Union ranks was America's top Catholic leader, a staunch Lincoln man who saw the dangers of secession and held firm. This was despite the opposition of many of the bishops of the church, especially those in the South.

On October 12, 1861, President Abraham Lincoln wrote to Archbishop "Dagger John" Hughes, the powerful Irish immigrant head of the New York Archdiocese, whose support Lincoln desperately needed.

Lincoln had defeated Hughes's preferred candidate, former New York governor William Seward, a renowned defender of immigrants, for the Republican nomination in 1860.

Indeed it was Seward's closeness to Hughes and his work on providing funding for Catholic education that was most despised by the Know-Nothing wing of the new Republican Party.

That connection to Hughes had likely cost Seward the nomination, even after he led Lincoln by a wide margin on the first count at the Chicago convention. Any truck with Catholics was too much for many delegates.

Now Lincoln, at the urging of Seward, was setting up his own link with Hughes, who supported Lincoln's decision to fight.

He wrote:

Rt. Rev. Sir: I am sure you will pardon me if, in my ignorance, I do not address [you] with technical correctness. I find no law authorizing the appointment of chaplains for our hospitals; and yet the services of chaplains are more needed, perhaps, in the hospitals, than with the healthy soldiers in the field. With this view, I have given a sort of quasi appointment, (a copy of which I inclose) each of three Protestant ministers, who have accepted, and entered upon the duties.

If you perceive no objection, I will thank you to give me the name or names of one or more suitable persons of the Catholic Church, to whom I may with propriety, tender the same service.

Many thanks for your kind, and judicious letters to Gov. Seward, and which he regularly allows me both the pleasure and the profit of perusing.

With the highest respect Your Obt. Servt. A. LINCOLN

Hughes had not asked about the chaplaincy positions, but Lincoln saw an opportunity to engage him. It was an example of how keen Lincoln was to have the spiritual leader of the Irish in America on his side. There were over a million Irish Catholics in America, many just off the Famine ships. Lincoln needed them for his depleted army.

Archbishop "Dagger" John Hughes (1797–1864) of New York was the key figure in the American Catholic Church during the Civil War, and the most important voice calling on the Irish to side with Lincoln. There was no shortage of voices urging the Irish to take the Confederate side, most notably John Mitchel, an 1848 revolutionary, who wrote eloquently of the plight of the Irish peasant but could never make the same connection to enslaved blacks.

Like Thomas Francis Meagher, Mitchel had escaped exile in Australia and had come to the US, but his moral direction deserted him as he threw in his lot with the slavery-supporting South. He derided Lincoln as "an ignoramus and a bore; not an apostle at all; no grand reformer, not so much as an abolitionist, except by accident—a man of very small account in every way."

The *Southern Citizen* newspaper that he set up in Memphis had a simple credo: "The Institution of Negro Slavery is a sound, just, wholesome Institution; and therefore, that the question of re-opening the African Slave Trade is a question of expediency alone."

He called blacks "an innately inferior people. . . . We deny that it is a crime, or a wrong, or even a peccadillo to hold slaves, to buy slaves, to keep slaves to their work by flogging or other needful correction." He wished to make the people of the US "proud and fond of [slavery] as a national institution, and advocate its extension by re-opening the trade in Negroes."

He based many of his beliefs on slavery on a two-thousand-mile trek through the South to observe it firsthand.

As *History Ireland* magazine noted in an article on Mitchel and his support for slavery in May 2007: "He particularly admired the South's gentility and old-world manners, claiming that on a journey of two thousand miles through the cotton states he had not heard a harsh word or seen a violent action."

The "peculiar gentleness of demeanor and quiet courtesy" of the South he attributed to slavery, which he believed had a restraining influence on the slave-owner because of the power and responsibility with which he was entrusted.

The Southern custom of speaking gently to servants and slaves created "'a softness of manner and tone which, in educated people, being united with dignity, and self-possession, gives me the ideal of a well-bred person.'"

With Irish of the prominence of Mitchel preaching Confederate doctrine, as well as the Southern Catholic bishops staying firm in support of the Confederacy, the position of Hughes was of paramount importance.

Bishop Lynch of Charleston, a friend of Hughes, positively endorsed slavery and kept ninety-five slaves of his own. He also condoned the rape of black girls by white men on the grounds that it kept white women pure. Archbishop Hughes was not of such a racist mindset. Years later, the two clerics would be sent on separate competing missions to woo the pope to their side.

Hughes from the beginning was beloved by his flock; the story of the gardener who became an Archbishop was the stuff of legend. He had come out of nowhere. Born on a tenant farm in Tyrone in 1797, he was hedge schooled (writer William Carleton was a schoolmate).

At age fifteen, Hughes was incensed when the family was refused the right to bury his sister in a Catholic grave with a priest present because of Ireland's penal laws. The best the priest could do was bless a handful of earth and pass it to young Hughes to sprinkle on the coffin. Many years later, Hughes said, he had dreamed of "a country in which no stigma of inferiority would be impressed on my brow, simply because I professed one creed or another."

He left for America, became a gardener in a church garden in Emmetsburg, Maryland, and was given a shot at the priesthood after several requests by the head of the seminary there.

He had a stellar rise, especially given the fact that he had no network of powerful clerics or wealthy families to help him. After he became Archbishop of New York, he was one of the most powerful clerics in the country, and he enjoyed a level of power and influence beyond any New York church leader before or since. He was universally known as "Dagger Hughes" because of the dagger-like way he portrayed the Holy Cross symbol on his letters. It was also said that he was known as "Dagger John" because of the the stiletto-like cross he wore.

He was personally vain, wearing a toupee to cover his baldness, but also personally very generous to those in need. From the beginning, he knew that anti-Irish sentiment was out there. (James Gordon Bennett, a leading editor, described Irish witnessing church rituals as the equivalent of "passing gold rings through pigs' noses.")

A Whig rather than a Democrat, Hughes had close Republican connections, especially with influential editor Thurlow Weed and

Seward. Seward remained one of the few American politicians partial to immigrants.

Those connections proved invaluable in framing Hughes's response to the outbreak of Civil War. Hughes was keenly aware that the Irish Catholics did not approve of slavery but cared little for the slavery issue, given their own concerns as a beleaguered group. The level of commerce with the South, especially cotton exports through New York Harbor, meant there was strong business sentiment for the Confederacy.

The arch-proponents of slavery in the North, such as Samuel Morse, August Belmont (though he later recanted), George Curtis, and Samuel Tilden (who would later be cheated out of the 1876 presidential election) were not Irish. They were mostly virulently anti-Catholic, too.

Despite those considerations, however, Hughes never hesitated in supporting Lincoln. Lincoln biographer Carl Sandburg notes that soon after war broke out "cheers and applause greeted the public reading of a letter of John Hughes, Archbishop of the Roman Catholic Church of New York, declaring for the Stars and Stripes: 'This has been my flag and shall be till the end.' At home and abroad, the Archbishop would have it wave 'for a thousand years and afterward as long as Heaven permits, without limit, of duration.'" It was hoisted over Old St. Patrick's Cathedral.

It was deeply important to Lincoln that Hughes went so public with his support.

Hughes could be a difficult, paradoxical character who carried more influence among his Irish flock than any churchman. But there was never any doubt he was in charge. Thus, an alliance was hugely important to Lincoln.

"It is an understatement to say that John Hughes was a complex character," wrote Monsignor Thomas Shelley, an expert on John J. Hughes. "He was impetuous and authoritarian, a poor administrator and worse financial manager, indifferent to the non-Irish members of his flock, and prone to invent reality when it suited the purposes of his rhetoric. One of the Jesuit superiors at Fordham with whom he quarreled said, 'He has an extraordinarily overbearing character; he has to dominate.'"

According to the *Catholic Encyclopedia*, "He was feared and loved; misunderstood and idolized; misrepresented even to his ecclesiastical superiors in Rome, whose confidence in him, however, remained unshaken. Severe of manner, kindly of heart, he was not aggressive until assailed."

Hughes never forgot he was an emigrant from County Tyrone; his family suffered massive injustice from the British, and he resolved to embrace his new country with all the passion and commitment he had once fit for Ireland before being driven out.

"I am an American by choice, not by chance," he once said. "I was born under the scourge of Protestant persecution, of which my fathers in common with our Catholic countrymen have been the victim for ages. I know the value of that civil and religious liberty, which our happy government secures for all." Lincoln was his man to ensure that continued.

Hughes was appointed coadjutor bishop in New York in 1838 and bishop in 1842; he was later named an archbishop. In 1844, Know-Nothing riots destroyed Catholic churches in Philadelphia. Hughes made clear he would not tolerate such atrocities in New York.

"If a single Catholic Church were burned in New York, the city would become a second Moscow," he said, referencing the scorched-earth policy Russia devised to block Napoleon. In addition, he placed armed Ancient Order of Hibernian guards around Old St. Patrick's Cathedral on Mott Street. The Know-Nothings slunk away after seeing the formidable army ready to fight them. "Dagger John" was not for trifling with.

In 1845, the first Irish famine survivors began trickling in, but it soon became a flood and then a tsunami. Hughes had the task of overseeing a massive increase in parishioners, most poor and starving, as well as a massive expansion of church schools, services, and charity.

Hughes had no illusion what he was dealing with. Eight hundred and fifty thousand destitute Irish arrived in New York City—one-hundred sixty-three thousand of them in 1851 alone. Samuel F. B. Morse, inventor of the telegraph, helped found the Native American Democratic Association, which was set up to stop emigration from Ireland, demanding a twenty-one year residency before immigrants could vote and barring from office anyone who "recognizes any allegiance or obligation of any description to any foreign prince, potentate or power"—i.e., the pope.

Hughes knew full well the scale of the problem and the hatred being aimed at his desperate flock.

The Know-Nothings were thriving in the wake of the foundering Whig Party, which was deeply split over slavery. At its height in the 1850s, the Know-Nothings elected more than a hundred congressmen and eight governors, and controlled six state legislatures and thousands of local politicians.

Like famed nativist Samuel Morse, they wanted a twenty-one year wait for citizenship and Catholics barred from office.

Know-Nothing riots against Catholics in Pennsylvania had fully alerted Hughes to the looming hate-filled attacks. The Know-Nothings even had their own fake "Protocols of Zion."

As Lorraine Boissoneault pointed out in *The Smithsonian Magazine,* an "exposé" published by one Maria Monk, "who claimed to have gone undercover in (a) convent, accused priests of raping nuns and then strangling the babies that resulted. It didn't matter that Monk was discovered as a fraud; her book sold hundreds of thousands of copies." Catholic churches were being attacked everywhere. Archbishop Hughes was under siege.

In New York, the arch villain was William "Bill the Butcher" Poole (played brilliantly by Daniel Day-Lewis in the *Gangs of New York* movie about the period). The conspiracies were so virulent that churches were burned, and Know-Nothing gangs spread from New York and Boston to Philadelphia, Baltimore, Louisville, Cincinnati, New Orleans, St. Louis, and San Francisco.

Bill the Butcher terrorized Irish voters at the polls. There was serious physical violence including murder attempts when they saw Irish casting votes. One man had had enough—John Morrissey, an Irish-born prizefighter and adventurer, who challenged Bill the Butcher. Their first fight was broken up, but the gangs later clashed and Poole was shot dead by a Morrisey gang member. Poole became the first Know-Nothing martyr.

No person exemplified the working class racist more than Poole. 250,000 people came to lower Manhattan for the wake, and leading politicians and dignitaries showed up for the psychopath's funeral.

Hughes knew his flock were terribly vulnerable. Slavery was an abstraction, mistreatment and attacks on his flock were not. "Most (Irish) move on across the country—those who have some means, those who have industrious habits," he observed. "On the other hand, the destitute, the disabled, the broken down, the very young, and the very old, having reached New York, stay. Those who stay are predominantly the scattered debris of the Irish nation."

The hatred of the new arrivals was intense. The diarist George Templeton Strong, for example, wrote that "the gorilla is superior to the Celtic in muscle and hardly their inferior in a moral sense." *Harper's* in 1851 described the "Celtic physiognomy" as "simian-like, with protruding teeth and short, upturned noses."

Hughes combated all that while employing a vast army of priests and nuns to minister to the massive number of new members of his flock. His priests emphasized personal responsibility. He started temperance societies, founded what is now Fordham University, and opened an emigrant bank.

He also saved thousands of women from prostitution, and worse. He laid the cornerstone for the new St. Patrick's Cathedral in what was then uptown New York, where there was consternation at the idea of dirty Catholics worshipping in the blueblood neighborhood.

Somehow Hughes thrived, and by the time of the Civil War out-break, he was by far the most important clergyman in America. He performed an invaluable service for Lincoln by urging Irish to enroll in the Union army.

He did so, however, clear in his mind that the reason the Irish enlisted had nothing to do with slavery, but rather with finally dis-proving the Know-Nothings and those who claimed that the Irish were unfit to serve. None could question the Irish man's patriotism after fighting for his adopted country, Hughes argued.

Hughes was keenly aware that Lincoln was deeply unpopular in Democratic New York; he lost the city heavily twice in elections.

That was not unconnected to the fact that the business of shipping cotton from the South through New York port was a $200 million yearly enterprise.

Author John Strausbaugh, an expert on New York history and politics, told author Dermot McEvoy on IrishCentral.com, "Principally, because of New York City's long and deep economic ties to the international cotton trade, the majority of New Yorkers saw it in their personal interests to support the South and plantation slavery. They saw Lincoln as the candidate of the abolitionists, and were convinced he'd move to end Southern slavery if elected—despite his saying, many times and in many ways, that he had no intention of doing so. Thus many New Yorkers were hostile to him. New Yorkers voted against him 2-to-1 in 1860 and again in 1864."

Strausbaugh had no doubt Hughes acted to help Lincoln despite having no argument with slavery. "He lashed abolitionism as a dangerous 'mischief,'" wrote Strausbaugh. Hughes seemed to waver in moral authority when confronted with the evil of slavery. "Because Catholicism was so beleaguered in America at the time," Strausbaugh told IrishCentral, "the Catholic Church was not very forthcoming about slavery, not wanting to make enemies on any side of the issue. The Church's basic stance, which Hughes espoused, was that so long as slavery was legal in the South, owning slaves was not a sin, though mistreating them was."

But Hughes remained crystal clear on the reason to back and support Lincoln as the freely elected president.

"If the country and the Government are not maintained by every sacrifice that is necessary to maintain them, then your United States will become a Poland—then it will become divided—then the strife will multiply across every border; every State or every section will claim to be independent and make itself an easy prey for those who will turn and appropriate the divisions of the people."

So despite the hatred expressed towards Catholics by many in Lincoln's party, Hughes saw that the Irish had no choice but to support him. Later, suspicious of Lincoln's tactics, Archbishop Hughes warned [Meagher] of a rumor in the city that Lincoln was really prosecuting the war to free the slaves; if it was true, [Hughes] said Irishmen 'will turn away in disgust from the discharge of what would otherwise be a patriotic duty.'"

CHAPTER THIRTEEN

Fighting for Lincoln:
General Michael Corcoran

The Irish Volunteer
When the Prince of Wales came o'er, and made a hubba boo,
Oh, everybody turned out, you know, in gold and tinsel too;
But then the good old Sixty-ninth didn't like these lords or peers
They wouldn't give a damn for kings, the Irish volunteers!
We love the land of Liberty, its laws we will revere,
"But the devil take nobility!" says the Irish volunteer!

General Michael Corcoran, the third Irishman who heavily influenced the Irish to fight for the Union, knew Lincoln personally, but he never undertook secret diplomatic missions for him, and neither would he become as famous as Thomas Francis Meagher or Archbishop Hughes.

But by one symbolic act, he became an instant Irish hero and the toast of Irish New York, and a magnificent recruiter for Lincoln.

Today, a statue to Corcoran stands just off a rural road in Ballymote, County Sligo. It was unveiled by New York Mayor Michael Bloomberg in 2014, and the statue shows Corcoran sitting astride a horse, riding towards battle perhaps; American and Irish flags fly proudly.

Bloomberg's speech is interesting and utterly anodyne, leaving out any reference to Corcoran's most famous act of refusing to march his Irish unit before the Prince of Wales during a visit to the US in 1860. Even in today's world, his advisors would clearly think it might be too personal.

Corcoran was arrested and held for court martial. The proceedings had actually begun when the Civil War broke out. The Know-Nothings and the WASP media pounced. The reaction was swift, flowing in from coast to coast, with every criticism of the Know-Nothings paraphrased as "What an insult to the monarch, those dreadful Irish, see they have no intention of showing loyalty to the US."

But his refusal to march and dip the flag made Corcoran an immediate hero. The Irish flocked to him.

Corcoran also had one major secret known only to a few. He was the top Fenian in America, ordained as such by Fenian founder John O'Mahony. The secret Irish army would ultimately attract tens of thousands of Irish, ready to use the Civil War as their learning ground for the much more important battle to drive the British out of Ireland. The Fenian leader Corcoran held powerful sway.

Irish Union soldiers may have been uncertain about their allegiance to Lincoln, but there was no question that on the issue of Irish freedom they were utterly united. The Famine had seen to that.

So Corcoran was much more than an Irish leader in the army. He was the top Fenian, the man among others plotting an invasion of Canada and forcing the British to concede Ireland in exchange for their Canadian dominion.

(That invasion of Canada actually took place after the Civil War on June 1, 1866 and after Corcoran had died. It was headed instead by General John O'Neill, with a thousand hardened Irish Civil War veterans. After defeating the British at the Battle of Ridgeway, O'Neill realized two other units and thousands of men had never crossed. He had won the only Fenian battle against the British ever, and he made an honorable decision to retreat. He later founded the town of O'Neill, Nebraska, and populated it with immigrant Irish. It exists to this day.)

When Fort Sumter was shelled and surrendered, Corcoran, a highly-prized military man, was suddenly freed and immediately set about raising an army to go south. Unlike Meagher, he had no fleeting doubts about where the right side lay. He was never a slave proponent, and the freedom of his beloved Ireland could be at stake. He developed a friendship with Lincoln who, as in the case of Hughes and Meagher, saw him as a valuable ally.

Meagher was convinced by Corcoran to be a Lincoln man. After a brief struggle with his conscience, as he had many friends in the South, Meagher joined up.

Corcoran was a marvelous recruiter for the Union. Five thousand applied to join him, although he was only looking for one thousand. Meagher was among them. The Irish Brigade and the Fighting 69th were coming to fight for Lincoln, no sure thing at the commencement of hostilities. It was great news for the Commander-in-Chief.

Corcoran was a friend of Meagher's who had also fled to the US after the 1848 Rising, although he was part of a different revolutionary group, the Ribbonmen, rather than the Young Irelanders.

Rail thin and standing well over six feet tall with a military bearing, Corcoran struck quite the figure. He joined the Revenue Police part of the British military machine, charged with closing down illegal drinking dens. He got the best military education the British could give.

The British were in relentless pursuit of the Ribbonmen, penniless tenant farmers in the Ulster area who organized secret meetings and targeted landlords throwing Irish peasants off their land. Corcoran, known universally as "Mick," was actually a double agent for the Irish side, after joining the British revenue police and reporting back all their activities to the Ribbonmen. He went on nighttime raids against rack-rent landlords while working for the British during the day. He must have been found out. Corcoran left Ireland abruptly, sailing out of Sligo Bay on August 30, 1849. He was clearly a man on the run.

After emigrating, Corcoran built a spectacular career in New York as a shrewd political operator who delivered the Irish vote. He achieved a patronage gift as a postal service senior staffer, and when war came, his background as a military man with his Irish experience resulted in him quickly climbing the ranks to colonel in the New York 69th militia.

Unlike many others, including Meagher and John Mitchel from the 1848 Rising, he never gave up on fomenting revolution in Ireland itself.

On October 11, 1860, came his moment of glory. He was the commander of an all-Irish unit that was asked to take part in a parade as part of a grand welcome to the then Prince of Wales, later King Edward VII.

Colonel Corcoran refused. "I cannot in good conscience order out a regiment of Irish-born citizens to parade in honor of a sovereign under whose reign Ireland was made a desert and her sons forced into exile," he said. "In the Prince of Wales, I recognize my country's oppressors." When asked to attend a military ball for the prince, he curtly responded, "I am not desirous to attend such a festivity." This added fuel to the fire.

The war intervened, and Corcoran rode off in a blaze of glory but was captured at the First Battle of Bull Run. Undaunted, he wrote from his prison cell, "One half of my heart is Erin's, and the other half is America's. God bless America, and ever preserve her the asylum of all the oppressed of the earth, is the sincere prayer of my heart."

After he was released as part of a prisoner exchange in 1862, he was invited to dine with Lincoln and begged him for a new command. He drew the biggest crowd of Irish ever assembled when he returned to New York a free man. His legend had only spread by his bravery at Bull Run and subsequently as a prisoner where he refused to be exchanged unless his men were, too.

With Lincoln's direct permission he formed Corcoran's Legion; the equivalent of six regiments signed up for him. They fought bravely and successfully in several key battles. "Never Retreated, Never Defeated" was their battle cry.

Alas, his life was cut short at age thirty-six when he fell off a high-strung horse (although some claimed he suffered a heart attack first) on December 22, 1863 in Fairfax, Virginia, where he was the commanding general. He was returning home to his house in Virginia, after accompanying Thomas Francis Meagher, who was headed to New York, to the train station. Meagher was due to pick up their wives and return with them to Virginia, and join Corcoran for the Christmas vacations.

Meagher was inconsolable. "There, in that very room I had occupied for several days as his guest . . . he lay cold and white in death, with the hands that were once so warm in their grasp, and so lavish in their gifts crossed up on his breast."

The task of helping Lincoln win the Civil War had just gotten much tougher.

CHAPTER FOURTEEN

Lincoln's Unexpected Heroes

The Transgender Hero

Clogherhead, County Louth, seems an unlikely place for an incredible aspect of American Civil War history to come from.

Abraham Lincoln's most famous transgender soldier and supporter hailed from the little hamlet. An estimated 400 women served as male soldiers in the Civil War, but only one, it seems, Albert Cashier, a.k.a. Jennie Hodgers from Clogherhead, spent her entire life as a man, unlike the others, who stepped back into their old identities.

Her story, from immigrant to hero soldier, to a life as a man, would be unbelievable even as a Hollywood fable.

She was the most exotic person to ever emerge from the little Irish fishing village which, while quaint, is not well known as a popular destination. Indeed, the nearby town of Drogheda, which Oliver Cromwell sacked, carries most of the weight of local history.

But something extraordinary did happen in Clogherhead with the birth of Jennie Hodgers on Christmas Day, 1843.

From an early age, though illiterate, Jennie planned a life away from grim pre-Famine Ireland.

Jennie left the Old World behind and shed her old identity to sail as a stowaway dressed in man's clothes to America. When she reached America, it has been posited that a male relative dressed her as a boy to get her a job working in a shoe factory, where the workforce was all male.

She arrived just as the Civil War broke out, and Abraham Lincoln had recently called for three hundred thousand volunteers. Jennie changed her name to Albert Cashier and volunteered for the 95th Infantry Illinois. She knew the medical exam merely looked at hands and feet, and an illiterate person could sign up.

She joined the Union army on August 6, 1862. At five foot three and slight in build, she ran the risk of discovery. Somehow she passed, and obviously whatever medical examination occurred was cursory.

She was soon in the thick of the fight. Her regiment took part in forty engagements, including the critical siege at Vicksburg masterminded by General Ulysses S. Grant, which proved a turning point in the war. She also took part in the battle of Guntown, Mississippi, where they suffered heavy losses.

She was captured while on a reconnaissance mission in Vicksburg. She managed to grab her captor's gun and knock him out and escape. On another occasion, she rescued her company's flag, an incredibly important symbol for every regiment. After the flag had been torn down, she rescued it, climbed a tree, and hung it from the highest branch.

Her bravery was unquestionable, but she was fortunate never to be injured or suffer any wound that would have necessitated a medical examination.

As for toilet facilities, there were none. Woods, trees, and forests provided enough privacy for her. Quoting Illinois Historical Society records, historian Jean Freedman wrote in *The New York Times* that "Hodgers's fellow soldiers recalled her as a modest young man who kept his shirt buttoned to the chin, hiding the place where an Adam's apple should be. Her comrades teased her because she had no beard, but this was an army of boys as well as men, and she was not the only beardless recruit in her company. She resisted sharing a tent with anyone, but made close friends among her fellow soldiers;

with one of them, she briefly owned a business after the war. Despite her diminutive size, she could 'do as much work as anyone in the Company.'"

On August 17, 1865, Jennie was mustered out of the army, having served her full three years.

As the County Louth genealogical records of her life noted, she witnessed some of the worst fighting in the war. "Starting from Camp Fuller, Rockford, near Chicago City in the north, her regiment would have moved south into enemy territory, through various States along the Mississippi River, to New Orleans along the Gulf of Mexico. At one point, in the Battle of Guntown, the whole regiment was nearly annihilated. Further recruiting took place at Memphis. In all, the regiment marched 1,800 miles, and moved, by rail and water, another 8,160 miles."

She returned to Illinois after the war, living as a man. She claimed her army pension and lived for forty years in the tiny town of Saunemin. Census records show several Irish families nearby. Her status as a man was never questioned. She lived alone and worked at various manual labor jobs. A local woman remembers Cashier rushing to her house during storms allegedly to calm down the kids, but the woman felt it was Cashier who needed comforting.

Every Memorial Day until 1910, she marched proudly with her fellow Civil War veterans in the military parade.

In 1910, her secret was first revealed after she was struck by an automobile and broke her leg. The doctor at the local hospital agreed to keep her secret safe, but advancing age and her leg injury meant she had to enter a veterans' hospital. Her mental health began to suffer, though she did manage to keep her secret for two years in the old veterans' home.

However, dementia and removal to a state hospital resulted in her secret becoming known. On March 29, 1914, *The Washington Post* reported on the woman who had posed as a man in the army. It went on to state the sad fact that Jennie was committed to an insane asylum, but reported how she'd "participated in some of the bloodiest battles of the war and behaved with gallantry."

At the asylum, she was forced to wear female clothing and came under investigation from the Pension Bureau, who wanted to remove her pension. It was then that her old comrades came to her rescue and saved her meager income.

Albert Cashier/Jennie Hodgers passed away on October 11, 1915, at the age of seventy-two. She was buried in her old uniform of the 95th Illinois Infantry and with full military honors in Sunny Slope Cemetery in Saunemin.

Back in her hometown, plans are still in motion to honor her, including a statue and a local event every year to remember her. Abraham Lincoln's most surprising soldier will not be forgotten. She answered the call from Lincoln and remains one of the most fascinating stories of the entire Civil War. In 1977, the people of Saunemin replaced the standard military marker on Jennie's grave with a much bigger one bearing the following inscription:

Albert D. J. Cashier
Co. G, 95th Inf. Civil War
Born: Jennie Hodgers
In Clogherhead, Ireland
1843-1915

Bridget Divers—Braver Than Any Man

Bridget Divers, known as "Irish Biddy," followed her husband into battle and was famous for dragging wounded soldiers to safety while under fire.

At the Battle of Fair Oaks she is said to have urged her husband's regiment, "Arragh go in boys and beat them and revenge me husband (who had been injured) and God be with ye."

Divers also often participated in combat. According to Mary Livermore, Sanitary Commission member and later a famed women's rights activist, "Sometimes when a soldier fell she took his place, fighting in his stead with unquailing courage. Sometimes she rallied retreating troops—sometimes she brought off the wounded from the field—always fearless and daring, always doing good service as a soldier."

Sometimes she even tried to turn around retreating Union soldiers, while at other times, she brought the wounded back to safety.

Charlotte E. McKay, a Civil War nurse, recorded meeting Bridget at City Point, Virginia on March 28, 1865:

Bridget—or as the men call her, Biddy—has probably seen more of hardship and danger than any other woman during the war. She has been with the cavalry all the time, going out with them on their cavalry raids—always ready to succor the wounded on the field—often getting men off who, but for her, would be left to die, and, fearless of shell or bullet, among the last to leave. Protected by officers and respected by privates, with her little sun burnt face, she makes her home in the saddle or the shelter-tent; often, indeed sleeping in the open air without a tent, and by her courage and devotion 'winning golden opinions from all sorts of people.' She is an Irish woman, has been in the country sixteen years, and is now twenty-six years of age.

Civil War nurse Rebecca Usher also remembered the fiery Irish woman:

A few days ago I saw Bridget, who came out with the First Michigan Cavalry, and has been with the regiment ever since. She had just come in with the body of a captain who was killed in a cavalry skirmish. She had the body lashed to her horse, and carried him fifteen miles, where she procured a coffin, and sent him home. She says this is the hardest battle they have had, and the ground was covered with the wounded.

She had not slept for forty-eight hours, having worked incessantly with the wounded. She is brave, heroic, and a perfect enthusiast in her work. Bridget said to me, in her earnest way, 'Why don't you ladies go up there, and take care of those wounded men? Why, it's the worst sight you ever saw. The ground is covered with them.' 'We should like to go,' I said, 'but they won't let us.' 'Well, they can't hinder me,' she said, 'Sheridan won't let them.'

She survived the war and was reputed to have headed out west to the new frontier. She certainly left in a blaze of glory.

CHAPTER FIFTEEN

Lincoln's Irish Soldiers— Captured by the Rebels

Author's Note: In the course of researching this book, I found to my utter surprise I had a relative, Dan Dowd, my great-great-grand uncle as far as I can tell, who fought and died fighting against slavery, for Lincoln and the Union. Thanks to brilliant research by Damian Shiels, his story has come to life. Dan Dowd lies in a marked grave at Andersonville National Cemetery near Atlanta, Georgia. His family had very hard times after his death, as the correspondence reveals.

Daniel and Mary Dowd were married in Dingle by Father Eugene O'Sullivan on October 29, 1853. The following year, on October 8, 1854, a child, Edward, was born.

Soon, the family emigrated to New York, arriving some time in the mid-1850s. In 1856, a daughter named Bridget, who would come to be known as "Biddy," was born on Long Island.

The family had settled in Buffalo by the 1860s, and on September 6, 1862, Daniel enlisted in the Union army, becoming one of around two hundred thousand Irish-born men who would fight in the war. He enlisted in the 155th New York Infantry, led by Brigadier-General Michael Corcoran from Carrowkeel, County Sligo.

Many Irish men in America chose to join Corcoran's brigade be-cause he was a known Fenian.

Daniel entered the army as a private in Company I of the 155th New York at Newport News, Virginia, on November 19, 1862. The records describe him as twenty-nine and a laborer, five foot five in height, with a fair complexion, gray eyes, and light hair.

His surname caused much confusion. He was placed on the regimental roster as "Daniel Dout," whereas in other places his name was recorded as Doud or Doody. These mistakes would come back to haunt his family.

By January, his regiment was engaged in the Battle of the Deserted House in Virginia. Daniel then spent the following year with his unit in Virginia. On December 17, 1863, he was guarding a railroad bridge, part of a detachment of around fifty men protecting the Orange & Alexandria line at Sangster's Station.

Sometime after 6:00 p.m., the detachment was attacked by a body of Confederate cavalry, who sought to burn down the bridge. The Rebels set fire to the regiment's tents and forced them into retreat. As the vastly outnumbered Union soldiers were cut off, the detachment would normally have looked to their telegraph operator to call for help, but he was apparently too drunk to be able to use his equipment.

General Corcoran and the rest of the unit did not learn of the attack until about 8:30 p.m., after a local Unionist informed them of the events. Although Union reinforcements were eventually sent and saved the bridge, a number of the Union men had been captured, including Daniel Dowd.

There is a small monument with the soldiers' names, including Daniel's, at the location where they fought so bravely.

Although there is little record of Daniel's life as a prisoner of war, he was most likely initially held near Richmond. In the spring or early summer of 1864, he was moved to the recently opened Camp Sumter in Georgia. Between February 1864 and the end of the war, nearly 13,000 prisoners died in the unsheltered compound, which was better known as Andersonville. Malnutrition, and therefore disease, was rife in the camp.

On July 3, 1864, Daniel, suffering from chronic diarrhea, was admitted to the hospital. He died before the end of the day. He now rests in Grave 2809 of the Andersonville National Cemetery. The warden, Henry Wirtz, was the only Confederate executed for war crimes.

Following his death, his widow Mary decided to leave the United States and return to Dingle with her children.

In 1869, while living on the Strand in Dingle, Mary, who was forty-five at the time, sought a US widow's pension based on her husband's service. She compiled information about her marriage and children and sent the application to Washington. However, Daniel's surname had been written as "Doody" in their marriage record, significantly different from the "Dout" recorded on the regimental roster.

In addition, there was no documentation relating to Biddy's birth. The Commissioner of Emigration wrote to every Catholic parish in Long Island for information, but nothing turned up. Unable to provide additional evidence, Mary's claim was classified as "abandoned" and she was denied the pension.

However, she never fully gave up. In her file is a letter sent by her in the 1890s to the Secretary of the Claim Agent Office at the White House in Washington, D.C.

The letter, addressed from Waterside, Dingle, on July 4, 1892, reads:

Sir,

I beg to state that I, Mary Dowd, now living here and aged about 65, am the widow of Daniel Dowd, who served as a soldier in the late American war of 1863, and died a Prisoner of War in Richmond Prison Virginia [actually in Andersonville, Georgia]. Said Daniel Dowd served in the Army of the North. After his death, I deposited the necessary documents to prove my title to pension, in the hands of a Mr. Daniel McGillycuddy Solicitor Tralee, with the view to place them before the authorities in Washington, and he on 27th December 1873, forwarded the same to a Mr. Walsh, a Claim Agent, for the purpose of lodging same. Since, I have not received a reply to my solicitor's letters or received any pay nor pension or acknowledgement of claim.

I also learn that my husband at his death had in his possession £100, which he left to Father McCooney who prepared him for death, in trust for me, and which sum never reached me.

I know no other course better, than apply to you, resting assured that you will cause my just claim to be sifted out, when justice will be measured to a poor Irish widow who is now working hard to maintain a long family.

Because Mary was illiterate, the letter was written for her by her solicitor, Daniel McGillycuddy. She signed it with an 'X.' It is unlikely she ever received any compensation from the US government.

The American-born Biddy grew up in Dingle, County Kerry, instead of the United States. She married a fisherman, Patrick Johnson, and they had seven children. She died in 1945 and is buried in St. James's Church in Dingle.

CHAPTER SIXTEEN

The Man They Couldn't Kill—
The Irish Medal of Honor Winners

Not only did the Irish come to fight for Lincoln, they came to fight well. "The Fighting Irish," in this context, is real.

The proof is there. The Medal of Honor, America's highest military honor, was created in December 1861 during the Civil War. It is the only US Military Award presented by the president in the name of Congress. The Irish own far more than any other foreign country. Historian Damian Shiels has identified 146 Irish-born Medal of Honor winners. There are likely more, he says.

The most remarkable honoree was "The Man They Couldn't Kill," Michael Dougherty, a private in the 13th Pennsylvania Cavalry from Falcarragh, County Donegal.

He won the medal for showing extraordinary bravery during an engagement with a Confederate regiment at Jefferson, Virginia, which saved an estimated 2,500 lives by preventing the Confederates from flanking the Union forces.

Dougherty had nine lives. He and 126 members of the 13th Pennsylvania Cavalry were later captured and spent twenty-three months in different Southern prisons, including the Andersonville death-camp in Georgia. He was the only survivor from his regiment.

His trials did not end there. Dougherty was heading for home on the steamship *Sultana* on the Mississippi River when the boilers exploded. Of the two thousand passengers, only 900 survived. Dougherty was one of them.

A large number of the medals were earned by Irish troops from Meagher's Irish Brigade, which fought and took heavy losses at Fredericksburg and Antietam.

CHAPTER SEVENTEEN

General Shields, Former Dueling Partner, Declares for Lincoln

There was another Irishman who might have been a candidate for the Medal of Honor. After surviving his near duel with Abraham Lincoln, Tyrone native James Shields went on to a remarkable legal, military, and political career—and an intriguing spy scandal. In 1843, he moved up from auditor general and became a judge on the Illinois Supreme Court.

Subsequently, Shields served for two years as a judge and then for a year as commissioner of the US General Land Office. On July 1, 1846, he was commissioned by President Polk as a brigadier general of volunteers to fight in the Mexican-American War, which began after Texas was annexed by the US from Mexico.

He served under future American president Zachary Taylor. Among those who fought with Shields in subsequent engagements in the war were a cadre of young officers such as Ulysses S. Grant, Robert E. Lee (who was directly under Shields's command), Stonewall Jackson, and George Pickett.

At the battle of Cerro Gordo, Shields received what many believed was a mortal wound, when a shot from a cannon felled him. He was assumed dead. After being struck, Shields was carried back to the medical tent by several soldiers, who thought they were bearing a corpse.

According to Richard Oglesby, an officer in one of the Illinois regiments, Shields regained consciousness and told him, "I am no further use to my country. You lay me down and let me die, for God's sake, lay me down and go to your duty." However, an Irish surgeon named McMillan, who ironically had been captured as he was fighting for the Mexicans, saved his life.

Shields came home a conquering hero and was given an appointment as governor of Oregon, a new territory. However, before he could take up the position, he ran for the Senate in Illinois and won. Though a Democrat, Shields opposed the extension of slavery, in a speech on the admission of California to the Union. He called slavery "a violation of natural law that can only be enforced by positive enhancement." He warned the South secession would fail because of it. "The South might as well attempt to shut out the pressure of the atmosphere as to shut out the whole pressure of the civilized world."

His term ended in 1855, and he ran again against Lyman Trumbull but was defeated. While in the Senate, he spoke passionately on Ireland and the fight against the British.

He resettled in Minnesota, where he had been awarded a large tract of land for his services. He had a dream that the wide-open state would be peopled by Irish exiles, and he ventured to New York but ran afoul of Archbishop Hughes, who wanted to keep his flock close. Nonetheless, Shields did persuade many Irish to come back to Minnesota with him. The town of Shieldsville, Minnesota, bears his name and was settled by Irish immigrants.

Shields soon involved himself in politics in Minnesota and amazingly, won a Senate seat in 1858 but only served one year.

He was still a major figure in Democratic Party politics and, but for being Irish-born, would surely have been a presidential contender.

He predicted correctly that the Buchanan presidency would be a disaster. While in Washington as best man for Stephen Douglas's wedding (his second), Shields stated of Buchanan, "The South elected him and will make him a Southern president. If he yields to this, he is lost."

Out of politics, the restless Shields set his sights for business reasons on booming California. In San Francisco in 1861, he married an Irish woman, Mary Carr, from County Armagh. The Shields and Carr families were close friends in Ireland.

When the Civil War broke out, Shields wrote to his old adversary and volunteered. Lincoln immediately made him a brigadier general. He was sent to the Shenandoah Valley in Virginia, the center of the fight for the Union.

The command of the Irish Brigade was originally intended for and offered to General J. Shields. Shields declined the offer, saying that "no one was so well entitled to the command as Colonel Meagher himself, who had raised the brigade, and shared the honors and perils of the first battle of the war with the gallant Sixty-Ninth."

Shields was soon to have his own appointment with destiny, facing the legendary Stonewall Jackson across a battlefield in Virginia in a famous encounter. In addition, a scandal involving him and a female Confederate spy was simmering.

CHAPTER EIGHTEEN

Taking on Stonewall Jackson, the Rebel Avenger

Stonewall Jackson was the Rebel avenger of the Civil War, a man who became so legendary that even Union prisoners rushed to hail him and cheer when he passed through the camp where they were being held.

Stonewall Jackson was descended from Robert Jackson, a farmer from Cumbria on the Scottish border with England. Jackson came to Ireland in 1609 as part of the Ulster plantation, replacing the rebellious Irish whose leaders had fled, taking their best land.

Unlike most of his cohorts who were Presbyterian, Robert was Anglican, a distinction that helped him advance enormously as it was the royal religion. He settled in Ballynarry, County Armagh, and fought several campaigns against the Irish who tried vainly to regain their lands.

Robert Jackson had two sons, John and Thomas. It was John who, in 1690, deflected the bullet which struck his gun and ricocheted off, hitting William of Orange at the Battle of the Boyne. Fighting on the other side were members of the Shields family.

John Jackson's son, also John, described as "a respectable and prosperous tradesman," and Stonewall's great-grandfather, emigrated to West Virginia in 1715, where he married an Englishwoman,

Elizabeth Cummins. Stonewall Jackson's father Jonathan, a lawyer, died young, as did his mother Julia. He was raised by relatives as a result.

There was a military tradition going back generations—his grandfather and great-grandfather had fought in the War of Independence.

Thomas Jonathan "Stonewall" Jackson, born in January 1824, went to West Point, graduating nineteenth out of a class of fifty-nine. After the Mexican War, he became an instructor of artillery at the Virginia Military Institute (VMI). In December 1859, he and a contingent of VMI soldiers stood guard at the execution of John Brown, the abolitionist who helped spark the Civil War.

When war broke out, Jackson joined the Rebels, breaking with his beloved sister Laura, who took the Union side. They never spoke again.

Jackson earned his nickname from the First Battle of Bull Run on July 21, 1861, when Brigadier General Barnard Bee, who was trying to rally his men, pointed to Jackson "standing like a stone wall."

Up to that point, Jackson had hardly made an impression. He was considered among the worst lecturers and odd to boot, often seen conversing with himself.

On the battlefield, however, he was transformed. There are those who believe that if Stonewall had survived his wounds at Fredericksburg, Lee would have won Gettysburg with Jackson at his side.

Jackson was a deeply devout soul. He was convinced that God was on his side against the rampaging Northern invaders. He believed in the message of Psalm 118: "The Lord is on my side, I will not fear." "Give them the bayonet" was his admonition to his men, as the enemy closed in on them.

In the campaign in the Shenandoah Valley, Jackson took on three separate federal forces and defeated them all. Forced marches, surprise maneuvers, brilliant reconnoitering, and best use of the topography saw Jackson became a legend. He drove his men hard, marching fifty miles in two days on one remarkable occasion. But he drove himself even harder.

Only once did he make a mistake—at the first battle of Kernstown, when his opponent was none other than James Shields. The two men, whose distant ancestors had faced each other at the Boyne, where Jackson's side had won a famous victory, would now fight again but with a different result.

Shields had orders from General Nathaniel Banks to pursue Jackson, who had retreated to the town of Strasburg. By the time Shields reached the town, Jackson was gone. A series of events followed as Shields, believing Jackson had fled, marched his Union army back east. On Jackson's side, false information given by his cavalry outriders made him underestimate severely how many soldiers Shields had in the field.

Jackson's cavalry now launched a surprise attack on Shields's forces, but the Irish veteran leading from the front fought him off at the cost of a broken arm for Shields, which took him off the battlefield.

Shields, now realizing Jackson was considering another attack, sent part of his force marching north, as if away from the battle. However, they were poised to return if Jackson attacked. It was a risky bluff.

The following day, Jackson advanced smack into the trap laid by Shields, believing from his cavalry intelligence that most of Shields's army had retreated. Jackson thought they would face a force of about three thousand instead of Shields's army, which numbered over ten thousand.

Jackson believed Shields and his replacement field commander, Nathan Kimball, were vulnerable on their right flank. Actually, the Union army had massive reinforcements ready to attack. When Jackson saw the actual size of the army, he told a subordinate "We are in for it," and so it proved at the Battle of Kernstown. It was a small battle and not decisively won, but because it was Jackson, it carried great weight.

Until the end of his life, Shields gloried in the fact that he was the only Union general to defeat Jackson in an open battle. There was even talk of Shields taking overall command of the army, or so Shields's supporters said. What happened, however, was quite the opposite. Weakened by his wounds, Shields was incapable of continuing to fight and resigned from the army, much to the chagrin of the Irish soldiers.

There is one mysterious coda to the life of James Shields. Karen Abbott, a *New York Times* best-selling author, wrote a book about real female spies in the Civil War entitled *Liar, Temptress, Soldier, Spy*.

In it, she claims Jackson's command of the Shenandoah Valley in one key battle was not entirely due to his military prowess.

She introduces us to Belle Boyd, an eighteen-year-old spy for the Confederacy who at one time, Boyd says, used her charms with the well-known ladies' man, General James Shields.

Shields stayed in the Fishback Hotel in Front Royal, where he had his headquarters during his Shenandoah campaign.

Belle, whose aunt owned the hotel, stayed in a cottage on the ground. She left her calling card and the fifty-one-year-old Shield "came running," to use Abbott's term. Belle told friends she found him charming: "He was an Irishman and endowed with all the graces of manner for which the better class of his countrymen are justly famous for."

During their frequent meetings, Belle pumped Shields for information. A visiting *New York Times* reporter stated that Belle "stayed four hours closeted with him" during his visit. She also had eyes for his aide-de-camp Captain Daniel Kelly. She apparently elicited from him the time and location of a gathering of Union generals at a council of war at the hotel.

On the appointed night, she managed to secure the room directly overhead where the meeting was being held and listened through a small hole in the floor. After the meeting, she dressed as a boy, mounted her horse, and rode past the Union pickets to Jackson's camp. Armed with the information, Jackson won an easy victory over federal forces the next day.

Some time later, a note arrived from Jackson himself. It read, "Miss Belle Boyd, I thank you for myself and for the army for the immense service that you have rendered your country today."

Did Shields spill any secrets, or was it Kelly, his aide de camp? Was Jackson greatly aided by the information? We will never know.

Amazingly, Shields had one more act—settling in Missouri where, yet again, he became a US Senator, the third different state and an unmatched achievement. As for Jackson, his war was soon over after Fredericksburg, where his own men shot him as he was returning to his lines, thinking him an enemy force. General Lee's army would never be the same. With Jackson by his side Gettysburg might well have turned out differently.

CHAPTER NINETEEN

Gettysburg, the Gap of Danger

There is a phrase in the Irish National Anthem, which is usually sung in Irish, that reads "Bearna Baol." The closest translation of "Bearna Baol" would be the "Gap of Danger," or the most dangerous part of the battlefield.

In Gettysburg on July 3, 1863, of all the one hundred seventy-five thousand or so men who had fought in the battle, it was the Pennsylvania Irish 69th who would face the fire of Pickett's Charge at its height.

Elsewhere in that battle, the climactic clash occurred as Pickett's Charge met the Union Blue front lines right in the center of the Union defensive line. There stood the men of the 69th Pennsylvania Brigade, immovable as other regiments ran.

They had no warning when they woke up that day of what would be their fate. The first two bloody days had been inconclusive, and both sides knew, given the massive loss of life and injuries suffered (around fifty thousand casualties between dead, wounded, and missing) that both armies were close to exhaustion.

On Wednesday, July 1, with the temperature a mild seventy-six degrees, the Rebels had the Union boys on the run even as both armies were still arriving. But the Union staved off disaster by retreating as far as the high ground on Cemetery Hill, a gently sloping ridge that gave the Union army the precious ability to look down on their opponents.

On July 2, with the temperature at eighty-one degrees, Lee flung his army at both flanks, but the Union held despite massive casualties. Now it was July 3 and a sweltering eighty-seven degrees. The soldiers in their heavy cotton military uniforms were close to heat exhaustion by midday.

It came down to this final test of strength. It is not fantasizing to say the fate of the Republic and what we now know as modern democracy, as well as the future of slavery, was at stake.

Lincoln stated it bluntly in his Gettysburg Address. The battle was critical in dictating whether "government of the people, by the people, for the people, shall not perish from the earth."

With a Confederate victory, the election of 1860 that put Lincoln in office would have meant nothing. Challenged by armed might, the United States would have split in twain with likely a military dictatorship in one or both jurisdictions. The popular vote would be overturned and useless.

The French had invaded Mexico and removed an elected leader, putting Emperor Maximilian in his place. The tide of anti-democracy was surging. The French were secretly helping the Confederates, sending thousands of weapons across the border.

If Lee had won at Gettysburg, a country founded on the back of slavery would have been created. The likelihood of British and French recognition of the new state would have almost definitely forced negotiation and peace on Confederate terms. Slavery as an institution would have been allowed to grow and expand.

Lincoln himself knew the stakes were at their highest. He told General Dan Sickles, who was injured badly and was a deeply controversial figure, that he knew Gettysburg was the turning point. The following quote is from Rufus Rockwell Wilson's book *Intimate Memories of Lincoln*:

"When Lee crossed the Potomac and entered Pennsylvania, followed by our army, I felt that the great crisis had come. I knew that defeat in a great battle on Northern soil involved the loss of Washington, to be followed perhaps by the intervention of England and France in favor of the Confederacy. I went to my room and got down on my knees in prayer."

If the Union lost, what did that mean for millions of black slaves? The massacre of black soldiers slashed and stabbed to death after they had surrendered to Confederate leader Nathan Bedford Forrest and his men at Fort Pillow in April 1864 showed what was in store for the black man in a Confederate state if Civil War generals ruled. "The river was dyed with the blood of the slaughtered," Forrest, who was one of the founders of the KKK, boasted.

Future events, such as the vital American intervention in two world wars, might likely have never happened if America had split in two. Europe might conceivably be under a Nazi dictatorship.

At Gettysburg, the Rebels reached the furthest point of their journey to force the North to offer terms and form their own country. Pickett's Charge was their last desperate lunge. It would be the high-water mark of the Confederacy.

An astute observer would certainly have bet on Lee, the magician who conjured victories against far greater numbers out of thin air and defeated the leaden-footed Union army again and again. However, he had lost his right-hand man Stonewall Jackson to friendly fire at Fredericksburg.

On the other side was an Irish American general who was commanding a major army for the first time. He had been notified only three days earlier that he was commanding general of the army of the Potomac, as Lincoln cast desperately around for a fighting general. How could such an inexperienced leader take on the tactical genius who led the Confederates?

General George Meade was suddenly center stage in the most important battle of the Civil War. His great-grandfather Robert Meade changed the family name from O'Meagh when he arrived from Ireland and settled in Philadelphia, where he became a strong supporter of the church and helped build St. Joseph's church there.

His daughter, Catherine, married an Irishman, Thomas Fitzsimons, who was one of two Catholic delegates who helped to frame the American constitution. Two of General George Meade's relatives were among the founders of the Friendly Sons of St. Patrick in Philadelphia.

General Meade, the unlikely hero of Gettysburg, was born in Cadiz, Spain on December 31, 1815, and baptized in the parish of Nuestra Señora del Rosario. The family eventually moved back to the United States and Meade graduated from West Point, fought in the Mexican War, became an army surveyor, and eventually took a commission of brigadier general when the Civil War blew up. His bold actions at Antietam and Chancellorsville marked him as a general who could fight even where the overall battle was lost. While others dithered, Lincoln rolled the dice with him.

So, on June 28, 1863, just days before the Battle of Gettysburg (July 1–3, 1863), after the forced resignation of ever-cautious General Joe Hooker, Meade was put in charge, much to his surprise. Meade said he didn't know whether the messenger from Washington had come to arrest him or promote him, so treacherous were Union army politics at the top.

It was an extraordinary rise, given his Irish Catholic background and the deep animosity radical Republicans and Know-Nothings held towards him. One of those radicals, Thaddeus Stevens, suspected Meade held Copperhead views, a faction of Democrats who wanted to sue for peace with the South on any terms.

His enemies, led by former army officer Dan Sickles who fled from Gettysburg, tried to prove Meade had mishandled the battle, a strange accusation given his side won. They even held joint committee hearings on Meade's handling of the war.

On day three, Lee made up his mind where his army would attack. Right at the center of the Union line was a copse of trees. That, Lee told his officers, was the target. In front of the copse was the 69th Pennsylvania Brigade, Irish to a man.

Amazingly, General Meade had outthought Lee on the vital matter of where he would strike. At eight that morning, he had sent a dispatch, saying it seemed to be the enemy's intention, "to make the attempt to pierce our center."

Journalist Whitelaw Reid described Meade as "calm" and ". . . lit up with the glow of the occasion."

The battle started with a massive cannonade from the Rebels. According to a veteran of the Philadephia 69th, "The air [was] filling with the whirring, shrieking, hissing sounds of the solid shot and the bursting shell. [The men threw] themselves flat on the ground behind the low stone wall." The firing from so many cannons sounded like a continuous roar, deafening and terrifying. The soldier recalled that artillery shot and shell "flew through the air high above us or [struck] the ground in front, ricocheting over us . . . [or smashed into] the wall, scattering the stones around."

The gunners were aiming much of their fire too high, however, and most of the balls passed over the Union line heads. The Union army artillery experts had prepared well. They had forty-one pieces of artillery, hidden by a small rise in the ground, which would prove vital.

Then came Pickett's march—thirteen thousand soldiers in serried file, marching their way across the open field to the Union lines about three-quarters of a mile away. They were cut down and enfiladed in massive numbers by the Union cannons and soldiers, but still marched straight towards the center of the Union line. It would take them fifteen to twenty minutes to cross the field. They were in plain sight as the cannon smoke disappeared.

The grim Union gunners eyed them well. There were shouts of "Fredericksburg" from the Union side, revenge for the death charge there in which the Irish Brigade, among thousands of others, had been cut to ribbons. Now, victory at Gettysburg would be their response.

Why did Lee order it? The most obvious answer is overconfidence after so many victories over superior numbers on the Union side. He believed his men were invincible. He learned the truth in a town eighty-five miles from Washington, a battle fought partly on the land of a freed slave.

Pickett's Charge was soon in sight of the Union defensive wall. They wheeled east and marched towards the copse of woods and the nearby gap that would forever be known as "The Angle."

Suddenly, a huge hole appeared in the Union line. The 59th New York had turned and bolted at the sight of thousands of Confederates bearing down. The Rebels pressed on. Next, the 71st Pennsylvania did the same. Remaining in the gap of danger were the Pennsylvania Irish 69th.

In the 69th, Colonel Dennis O'Kane called his men together and put steel in their soul. He warned his men not to fire until they "could distinguish the whites of their eyes," and above all he reminded them that they stood defending the very state they loved so much and a Union that had given a million Irish a new chance at life.

O'Kane told them that if any man should flinch in his duties, "he asked that the man nearest him would kill him on the spot." O'Kane, born in Derry, married and had two kids there before setting out for America, but he bled Union blue.

"These addresses were not necessary," wrote Private Anthony McDermott, "as I do not believe that there was a soldier in the Regt. that did not feet that he had more courage to meet the enemy at Gettysburg, than upon any field of battle in which we had as yet been engaged, stimulus being, the fact that we were upon the soil of our own State."

The 69th was the only regiment not to withdraw from defending the stone wall in front of the copse of trees during Pickett's Charge. Over the two days they fought at Gettysburg, they lost 143 men out of 258 who marched on to the battlefield on the second day.

O'Kane kept his men down behind the wall, controlling their instinct to fire at long range at their enemies. When the thousands of Confederates reached the Angle, they were convinced they could breach the Union defense and split the Union army in two. When they were only a few dozen yards from the wall, O'Kane ordered his men to jump up and open fire. Pickett's men were "staggered" and thrown into "disorder."

The Irish had armed themselves well, taking the rifles of dead soldiers and continuously firing as a result, not needing to reload.

The Confederates finally breached the wall led by one of their heroes, General Lewis Armistead. Now it was firing at point-blank range, ferocious fighting over control of the cannons, and finally, desperate hand-to-hand fighting and using their weapons as clubs. The Irish gave as good as they got. The heroic O'Kane was wounded and died later, but his men fought on until, at last, help arrived.

Two other Pennsylvania regiments now rushed to the defense of the Irish and one of their members shot Armistead dead as he tried to rally his men. Without their famed leader, the Rebels were whipped and disorganized. The Union center would not be breached.

Armistead, who had been present at the Hancock house in Los Angeles when "Kathleen Mavourneen" was sung as a tragic farewell, died only a short distance away from where his oldest friend Winfield Scott Hancock was playing a hero's role in leading the resistance against the Confederate onslaught.

Doctor Earl Hess, a leading historian of Pickett's Charge, writes that a turning point in the battle was the repulsion of Armistead and his thousands because "the 69th refused to give way. . . . This regiment put up a magnificent fight that saved the Angle and killed any chance that Pickett's division might push the Federals off Cemetery Ridge."

General Meade savored the victory as well he should have and wrote to his wife: "It was a grand battle and is in my judgment a most decided victory."

However, the strain might almost have been too much for him. He also mentioned that their son, also George, an aide to him, was fine but as for himself, "I feared I should be laid up with mental excitement."

For Robert E. Lee, it was a crushing defeat. It hardly helped that his principal subordinate General James Longstreet had warned him the morning of July 3 that "It is my opinion that no fifteen thousand men ever arrayed for battle can take that position," and he pointed to Cemetery Hill.

As for President Lincoln, he had double reason to celebrate after news that General Grant had taken Vicksburg, which gave the Union control of the vital Mississippi river.

Shortly after, Lincoln attended a prayer ceremony in Washington where a local Methodist bishop, who had been imprisoned in the notorious Libby prison in Richmond, told him that when news of Meade's victory had reached them, the whole prison erupted in wild celebration. Then, every prisoner sang the "Battle Hymn of the Republic" in unison.

A choir at the prayer event then broke into the song, and Lincoln, deeply affected, asked them to sing it again. The Republic had been saved from dissolution at Gettysburg, led by an Irish American general and featuring extraordinary courage by Irish immigrants.

CHAPTER TWENTY

Father Corby Summons God— The Draft Riots Cometh

The Irish heroics at Gettysburg were not confined to the Pennsylvania 69th. Colonel Paddy O'Rourke of the 140th New York, an Irish immigrant, had led his men on a breakneck charge to secure Little Round Top. The Maine 20th, under Joshua Chamberlain, had won back the fiercely disputed hill, which was a key element of the battlefield topography. If the Confederates could grab it, they would be able to overlook the Union position.

Chamberlain's men were in dire straits when O'Rourke and his men arrived and commenced their charge. The Texas and Alabama troops they faced thought they had won the day until the 140th counterattack began.

O'Rourke fell early in the battle when a Southern shooter brought him down with a bullet in the neck. However, his men arrived in time to help save Little Round Top for the Union, one of the key battles at Gettysburg.

Finally the Irish Brigade and their pastor, Father William Corby, wrote themselves into history. His passionate defense of the Irish Catholic soldiers he rode beside, prayed beside, slept beside, watching as they fought and died, is worth repeating. Nothing irked him as much as the anti-Catholicism he so often experienced.

He knew that despite the supreme sacrifice by so many Irish, they were still mocked and humiliated in the Eastern establishment and Know-Nothing world.

He wrote in his diary:

> Well nigh on every page of the history of the United States you find recorded the brave deeds of Irish Catholics, and Catholic of all nations, including American Catholics, who labored zealously in the cause of American liberty; and still we have the mortification of hearing, through the press, from the pulpit, and even in legislative halls, the hue and cry: 'Catholics will destroy our free institutions!'
>
> Did not Catholics furnish the material to make them? Shame on bigots for their ingratitude. . . . Shame on bigots for vomiting out spleen on the very men who . . . won for them, on bloody battlefields, the liberty they now enjoy. Hold! Enough!

On the second day at Gettysburg, Corby became famous far and wide for his deed. He was with his men when they were called into action in the area known as the Wheatfield, where a Union division was in difficulty. As the 600-member Irish Brigade and thousands of others filed down a narrow path to enter the battlefield, Father Corby jumped on a nearby rock and pronounced a general absolution on those who were heading for what might well be their last moments on earth.

Corby's stentorian tones competed with the sound of battle, but thousands fell to their knees and prayed with him.

"For Catholics at least, no event during the Civil War bound together Catholic and Protestants fully or united Catholics more with the nation then the moment when soldiers of all faiths knelt before Father Corby on the dawn of the second day of Gettysburg," posited Randall L. Miller, co-editor of *Religion and the American Civil War*, who has written very impressively on the issue of how the Irish contribution to Lincoln winning the Civil War has been overlooked.

A witness to Corby's remarkable speech wrote, "The scene was more than impressive, it was awe inspiring. Nearby stood a brilliant throng of officers, and there was profound silence in the ranks of the Second Corps. I do not think there was a man in the brigade who did not offer up heartfelt prayer. . . . Some knelt there in their grave clothes. . . . Father Corby pronounced the words of the general absolution."

The moment has passed into history, and Corby's statue stands proudly in Gettysburg and in Notre Dame where he had joined the Union army from and later served two terms as president. With that statue, Catholics entered American sacred space and memory.

Gettysburg in many ways was the demise of the old Irish Brigade. The Wheatfield battle went well for the Irish at first, but they were later driven back by sheer weight of numbers and suffered terrible casualties. Within a year, the original Irish Brigade was merged with other regiments.

After massive Union losses at Gettysburg, the draft proved an explosive issue. Most Irish were incensed at the belief they were being targeted as cannon fodder. However, with the enactment of the draft in 1863, Hughes preached a sermon urging that "volunteering continue and the draft be made; if three hundred thousand be not enough this week, next week make a draft of three hundred thousand more. The people should insist on being drafted, and so bring this unnatural strife to a close."

Hughes, however, had misjudged the anger over the draft issue badly, an uncharacteristic mistake by him.

Perhaps he was worn out by war and just wanted it over. He was also ill and close to death. The draft riots, the most shameful episode in Irish American history, came at the very end of Hughes's life. Irish Americans were enraged by the fact that the rich could buy their way out of conscription with three hundred dollars, an impossible sum that represented about a half year's salary for most working Irish.

The first names of those to be drafted were released on July 12, appearing in the *New York Herald* newspaper and breaking a promise by Governor Horatio Seymour, who had stated he would fill the

New York quota with volunteers and failing that, go to court to stop conscription.

The draft numbers from New York would be significant. By the end of 1862, it was reported that New York State was short 28,517 in volunteers, of which 18,523 were to be recruited in New York City.

It was the last straw for many. The horrendous casualties at Gettysburg left many an Irish family in New York bereft of their breadwinner, and the war had become increasingly unpopular. Now, thousands more of their menfolk were to be drafted, and many to die, in order to end Negro slavery.

Ironically, the draft notifications came on the July 12 weekend, when Orangemen celebrated and tensions were already high.

On Monday morning, the die was cast. The mob burned draft offices, destroyed telegraph wires, and assaulted police officers. It only went downhill from there.

As the riots went on, they took most of their venom out on the unfortunate blacks they encountered. Over 120 were killed, and the Colored Orphanage Asylum was destroyed in an act of pure savagery. Eleven black men were lynched. The great work of Meagher, the Irish Brigade, Michael Corcoran, and Hughes in bringing the Irish into the mainstream and making them no longer targets of hate was seriously undermined.

Hughes was deeply impacted but moved slowly—far too slowly. After the fury of the riots had somewhat alleviated, a gravely-ill Archbishop Hughes, dying from Bright's disease at age sixty-six, addressed his people, desperately trying to stop the carnage:

> Men! I am not able, owing to the rheumatism in my limbs to visit you, but that is not a reason why you should not pay me a visit in your whole strength. Come, then, tomorrow, Friday at 2 o'clock to my residence, northwest corner of Madison Avenue and Thirty-Sixth Street. There is abundant space for the meeting, around my house. I can address you from the corner balcony. If I should not be able to stand during its

delivery, you will permit me to address you sitting; my voice is much stronger than my limbs.

I take upon myself the responsibility of assuring you, that in paying me this visit or in retiring from it, you shall not be disturbed by any exhibition of municipal or military presence. You who are Catholics, or as many of you as are, having a right to visit your bishop without molestation.

Five thousand showed up the next day to hear a weak but strong-willed Hughes demand an immediate end:

Men of New York. They call you riotous but I cannot see a riotous face among you . . . . I have been hurt by the reports that you are rioters. You cannot imagine that I could hear these things without being pained grievously. Is there not some way by which you can stop these proceedings, and support the laws, of which none have been enacted against you as Irishmen and Catholics? . . . Would it not be better for you to retire quietly?

Hughes's words calmed the situation and played a major role in ending the riots. But it is a mystery why he did not move sooner.

"As for the draft riots," says Strausbaugh, "[Hughes] was treading a fine line. Other New Yorkers were blaming the Irish for the riots. He didn't want to play into that, but at the same time he wanted to discourage his flock from participating. It left him in rather a quandary, simultaneously denying the Irish had participated and asking them to stop."

Lincoln had earlier in the war wanted to parlay Hughes's massive influence abroad.

The archbishop's pro-Union stance meant he suffered much criticism, especially from Southern Catholic clergy and bishops. Lincoln saw an opportunity to defend Hughes and bulwark his support. He wrote to the Vatican about Hughes saying he "would feel particular gratification in any honor which the Pope might have it in his power to confer upon him." Was Lincoln suggesting that Hughes should be made a cardinal? His intent remains unclear.

They certainly had become close. Hughes was called to the White House and asked by Lincoln to act as an ambassador abroad, especially to the Vatican and Europe, where most of the monarchies expressed support for the Confederacy.

Hughes agreed to go on condition that Thurlow Weed, a close friend and a Republican who was a newspaper publisher, go with him.

Before Hughes embarked, Lincoln called him to Washington again. White House staff who saw the archbishop enter Lincoln's office speculated on what the conference was about. The prelate came out, entrusted with a secret mission. He knew that he was going to Europe—France, Spain, Italy—the Catholic countries. "Neither the North nor the South knew my mission," Hughes wrote a friend. "I alone knew it." Hughes did a sterling job and was received warmly at the Vatican. He persuaded several royal houses to remain neutral and established himself as a very high-profile Lincoln supporter.

Lincoln knew the situation on the international scene was perilous, which is why he needed Hughes, the uncrowned leader of the Catholic Church in America, to especially visit the Catholic leaders.

European leaders preferred a weak and divided nation on the American continent. In September 1861, England's former colonial secretary Sir Edward Bulwer-Lytton stated that a permanent division of the United States would benefit the "safety of Europe." A truly united United States "hung over Europe like a gathering and destructive thundercloud . . . [but] as America shall become subdivided into separate states . . . her ambition would be less formidable for the rest of the world."

"Dagger John" was aware of President Lincoln's concerns: "My mission was and is a mission of peace between France and England on the one side, and the United States on the other. . . . I made it known to the President that if I should come to Europe it would not be as a partisan of the North more than of the South; that I should represent the interests of the South as well as of the North; in short, the interests of all the United States just the same as if they had not been distracted by the present civil war."

Lincoln biographer Carl Sandburg wrote that "the Archbishop became one of the President's personal agents with full powers to set forth the Union cause in Europe. The Archbishop had interviewed the French Emperor, attended a canonization of martyrs in Rome, laid the cornerstone of a new Catholic university in Dublin built partly from moneys collected in America. In this tour of eight months over Europe the Archbishop spoke the pro-Northern views which he gave in a published letter to the pro-Southern Archbishop of New Orleans."

However, Hughes, ever wary of the WASP hatred of Catholics, refused to side with them on abolition. As for the Emancipation Proclamation, Hughes regrettably wrote a statement read at Mass: "We, Catholics, and a vast majority of our brave troops in the field, have not the slightest idea of carrying on a war that costs so much blood and treasure just to gratify a clique of Abolitionists in the North."

It seemed his hatred of the British and their New York equivalents, the Know-Nothings, blinded him to the horror of slavery as he focused relentlessly on building the Irish up so they could never be accused of being unpatriotic again.

The archbishop died on January 3, 1864. On January 13, President Lincoln paid fulsome tribute to Hughes in a letter to William Starr, administrator of the Diocese of New York:

Having formed the Archbishop's acquaintance in the earliest days of our country's present troubles, his counsel and advice were gladly sought and continually received by the Government on those points which his position enabled him better than others to consider. At a conjuncture of deep interest to the country, the Archbishop, associated with others, went abroad, and did the nation a service there with all the loyalty, fidelity, and practical wisdom which on so many other occasions illustrated his great ability for administration.

When John Hughes died, he left an incredible Catholic legacy. "When he came to New York in 1838, the diocese was ten times the size of the present-day Archdiocese of New York," wrote Monsignor Thomas J. Shelley. "It included all of New York State and the northern half of New Jersey, an area of fifty-five thousand square miles, with about two-hundred thousand Catholics. In that extensive diocese there were only 38 churches and 50 priests, two Catholic schools and a few orphan asylums. There was not a single Catholic college, seminary, rectory, hospital, or other institution."

Then came the Famine. "This rapidly growing Catholic population created an insatiable demand for more churches, schools, and charitable institutions," Shelley wrote. "In 1859, Archbishop Hughes boasted that he had dedicated ninety-seven churches in the previous twenty years, an average of one new church every ten weeks. In the area that remained part of the archdiocese, he established no fewer than sixty-one new parishes." In August 1858, Archbishop Hughes laid the cornerstone for the landmark St. Patrick's Cathedral on Fifth Avenue.

Hughes's role in the draft riots will be forever criticized, and rightly so. Perhaps he saw it as much more complicated than just Irish rioting.

The riot, said one writer, was "neither a Catholic insurrection nor a Catholic plot. The rioters being mostly Irish immigrants were, of course, Catholic. . . . But most of the police were Irish, too, and Catholic, and no police have ever worked harder or stood more resolute in the face of danger or showed more courage or devotion to duty than the police during those first three terrible days."

One rioter actually wrote to *The New York Times* explaining his position: "You will no doubt be hard on us rioters tomorrow morning but that $300 law has made us nobodies, vagabonds, and cast outs of a society for whom nobody cares when we just go to war and be shot down. We are the poor rabble and the rich rabble is our enemy by this law. . . . Why don't they let the N . . . kill the slave-driving race and take possession of the South[?]"

History has judged Hughes harshly but correctly on the abolition of slavery and the draft riots, but Lincoln could have no complaint with the Irish archbishop as a seminal figure who called on the Irish to fight for the Union and the president many of them despised.

This was despite strong opposition from within his own church and the business community, as well as many pro-Southern newspapers.

But Hughes did not lack courage in that respect. Like Lincoln, he was fearless in pursuit of what he thought was right. Their partnership played a vital role in the Union success in the Civil War.

CHAPTER TWENTY-ONE

The President Pardons Some Irish, Not Others

Lincoln could show an unsympathetic face to the Irish, too. The draft riots, not just in New York, caused problems for Lincoln. Lincoln wanted 17,000 men from Pennsylvania, and the Molly Maguires, the militant Irish group working in dreadful mining conditions, were a clear target for recruitment.

On October 16, 1862, the draft list was published, and an initially peaceful protest became violent, involving many of the Molly Maguires. Unable to end the violence, Colonel Alexander McClure, friend to the president, asked Lincoln if the recruits could be openly lied to and told when they turned up for duty that the list was filled, which was not the case. Lincoln quietly agreed.

Shortly after the draft riots in Philadelphia, as remembered by doorkeeper Thomas Pendel, grandson of an Irish immigrant, an entire Irish family arrived for a petition hearing on the case of two breadwinners who were in jail after the riots. The jailed men were clearly Molly Maguire members who had taken part in the violence.

Lincoln listened, stone-faced. Pendel recounts the conversation thus from the two Irish ladies, described as "tall, gaunt women" speaking in broad Irish accents:

"Howdy, Mishter president. We've come to see yes sir, to see if yers wouldn't pardon our men out of prison, sir."

Pendel noted, "This was said in whining, woe-begone voices and well-tended looks of despair on their faces."

The women continued. "We would like to have yers pardon 'em out of prison sir, so as to help support us, sir."

Pendel writes, "The president sized them up. He was a great reader of nature."

Then, in what must have been a patronizing Irish accent he replied.

"If yers husbands had not been resisting the draft they would not now be in prison; so they can stay in prison."

Lincoln was capable of great kindness, too. Pendel says another Irish woman with her young daughter got an audience with the president.

Pendel recounts the conversation thus: "Mr. President, my husband is down sick in Fredericksburgh, and I would like to have him discharged for I have my husband and two sons, all three in the army and I need the help of one of them."

The president said, "You make an affidavit to that effect and bring it back to me." Lincoln was signaling that he trusted her and was not going to check the truth of her story with the relevant army records.

Three weeks later the mother came back, however, and said by the time she got to the hospital, her husband was dead.

"Now I have two sons, yet. I want to see if you don't discharge one to help me get along and you can have the other one."

The president repeated the request that she give a signed affidavit and immediately promised to get one son back to her.

The Irish woman stepped closer to the president. "Mr. President, may God bless you and may you live very long years."

Afterward, Pendel recounts, Lincoln looked him straight in the eye and remarked, "I believe that old woman is honest."

Lincoln encountered opposition from his own generals over his liberal pardon policy. Father William Corby, the iconic chaplain of the Irish Brigade whose benediction to the troops marching to the battlefield at Gettysburg has gone down in history, recalled an extraordinary meeting with the president and, later, Lincoln's commanding general at Gettysburg, George Meade.

The case involved a thirty-two-year-old Irish-born soldier named Thomas Dawson from the 19th Massachusetts regiment. Prior to emigrating, Dawson had served in the British Army and won the Victoria Cross, according to his clemency petition.

In April 1864, he was sentenced to die after he and two companions left camp and broke into a house, where they drank liquor they found there. He claimed to have blacked out but was arrested the next day and charged in the rape of a sixty-year-old woman.

Dawson asked for Corby to meet his spiritual needs.

It was soon obvious that Dawson was considered an excellent soldier by his own officers. All of them signed an appeal document, a highly unusual occurrence.

Corby was dispatched to the White House to make the case with Lincoln. After being ushered in and greeted warmly by the president, he made his case.

Lincoln, it was clear, found it a hard case to offer a pardon in. Despite his best efforts, Corby knew he was falling short; the crime was unacceptable to Lincoln.

Corby tried one last gambit, stating, "Since Your Excellency sees fit not to grant it (the pardon), I must leave his life in your hands."

As Corby wrote, "This was too much. His (Lincoln's) tender heart recoiled when he realized that a man's life depended on his mercy.

"As I started across the green room to take my departure, he turned his own chair and throwing one of his long legs over the other said, "Chaplain, see here! I will pardon him if General Meade will, and I will put that on the petition."

Corby departed, happy with the outcome, but Meade could not be convinced. It was obvious he felt Lincoln was too soft-hearted on such issues.

"Father, I know Meade said your mission is one of charity, but sometimes charity for a few means cruelty for many. . . . Besides, the president should have given the final and positive decision. I will not act."

Thomas Dawson went to his death a few days later. He was one of three Irishman hanged for rape on the Union side out of a total of twenty-four.

CHAPTER TWENTY-TWO

Fear of Black/Irish Coupling Derails Lincoln Support

The polyglot nature of New York in the mid-1800s meant that many people and races who had never set sight on each other were now cheek by jowl in the slums.

Historian Lisa Orr wrote in *The New York Times* that black/Irish couples were far more common than many believed. Living side by side meant that it was inevitable that areas like the Five Points would feature multicultural relationships, the likes of which America had never seen.

A reporter for a New York paper in the 1830s lamented the "white women, and black and yellow men, and black and yellow women, with white men, all in a state of gross intoxication, and exhibiting indecencies revolting to virtue and humanity." Orr wrote that "harmonious or not, most mixed-race marriages in New York were between Irish women and black men, and mulatto children were common." The year 1850 saw a new racial category, mulatto, added to the census, to account for their offspring.

When the draft riots came, during a heat wave in the bleak middle of the Civil War, the mob that poured out of Irish neighborhoods were incensed they were being drafted while others escaped.

The mob targeted mixed-race households, especially those containing Irish women who had children with African American men.

Using crude racism even for the times, opponents of Lincoln saw the perfect opportunity to counter the backing of men like Archbishop Hughes, Thomas Francis Meagher, and Michael Corcoran by tying Lincoln directly to this dreadful crime they called "miscegenation." Their preferred weapon of choice was what we call today "fake news."

"Abraham Africanus" they called him, in the form of an influential pamphlet, the Facebook of its day, put about by "Copperhead" Democrats obsessed with ending the war by conceding the union. In the pamphlet, Lincoln does a pact with the devil to stay in power. The illustration of him shows him with a dark-skinned, goat-like visage.

A new word, "miscegenation," was invented, a description of blacks and whites coupling. The pamphlet purported to be written by abolitionists who supported mixed-race couples. The real intent was to frighten the Irish off Lincoln forever.

The pamphlet stated, "The word is spoken at last. It is Miscegenation—the blending of the various races of men—the practical recognition of the brotherhood of all the children." Just a year after the Emancipation Proclamation, it was calculated to further madden the anti-Lincoln voters.

A year later, a similar pamphlet appeared in New York. It had a very specific purpose, to drive Irish away from Lincoln by creating an appalling vista of black men and Irish women "miscegenating."

It was entitled *Miscegenation: The Theory of the Blending of the Races, Applied to the American White Man and Negro,* and it came out just as the 1864 election was looming large and the Civil War outcome was still uncertain.

Again, it purported to be an approving account of black/white breeding, but it very nakedly targeted the Irish as the ones whose women would most quickly desert them.

The pamphlet declared, "When the President proclaimed Emancipation, he proclaimed also the mingling of the races"; this was the killer blow the writers hoped to strike in forcing any Irish away from Lincoln.

The pamphlet advocated miscegenation between the Irish and blacks in order to strengthen the race.

"While science has demonstrated that the intermarriage of diverse races is indispensable to a progressive humanity, its votaries, in this country at least, have never had the courage to apply that rule to the relations of the white and colored races." The pamphlet told the Irish that "notwithstanding the apparent antagonism which exists between the Irish and Negroes on this continent, there are the strongest reasons for believing that the first movement towards [interracial marriages] will take place between these two races." The pamphlet added, "Indeed, in very many instances it has already occurred." Miscegenation balls between blacks and Irish were envisaged in illustrations—there were even portraits of Lincoln graciously welcoming black men and women to such events.

"Wherever there is a poor community of Irish {here} they naturally herd with the poor negroes, and as the result of the various offices of kindness which only the poor pay to one another, families become intermingled and connubial relations are formed between the black men and white Irish women."

The pamphlet warned, however, that Irish women would find Negro men irresistible. "The white Irish Woman loves the black man, and in the old country, it has been stated, that the Negro is sure of the handsomest among the poor white females."

The fake "abolitionist, Lincoln supporters" who wrote the pamphlet went on to insult the Irish in ferocious terms.

"Why the Irish were lower than the Negro," a "more brutal race and lower in civilization than the Negro" so that it would actually help the Irish to have sexual relations with blacks. "Fusion, whenever it takes place, will be of infinite service to the Irish. The Irish are coarse-grained, revengeful, unintellectual, with very few of the finer instincts of humanity."

The pamphlet even claimed the Irishman was actually black:

[He] was originally of a colored race, and has all the fervid emotional power which belongs to a people born in or near the tropics. His long habitation north, however, and the ignorance in which he has been kept by misgovernment, have sunk the Irishman below the level of the most degraded Negro.

Take an equal number of Negroes and Irish from among the lowest communities of the city of New York, and the former will be found far superior to the latter in cleanliness, education, moral feelings, beauty of form and feature, and natural sense.

One of the evidences of degeneracy which has been pointed out in certain of the Negro races has been the prognathous skull, the projecting mouth, the flat and open nostril. Yet this is a characteristic as true of certain portions of the people of Ireland as of the Guinea African. The inhabitants of Sligo and Mayo, portions of Ireland under peculiarly bad government, have developed these precise types of feature. The people have become thin-legged, pot-bellied, with mouth projected, head sloped, nostril distended; in short they exhibit all the characteristics by which we have marked the lowest type of the Negro.

It was dirty politics at its worst but even with the loss of New York, Lincoln emerged victorious. He had secured another term, the draft riots were quelled, and the Union army—with many newly-arrived Irishmen swelling its ranks—was winning the war.

CHAPTER TWENTY-THREE

The South Seeks to Stop Irish Migration

On September 4, 1863, not long after Gettysburg and with the tide of battle turning, a Confederate Irish-born chaplain, Father Patrick Bannon, received an urgent missive from Judah Benjamin, Secretary of State for the Confederacy. This came following a meeting Benjamin had with Jefferson Davis, president of the Confederacy:

> Sir:
> The Secretary of War having relieved you temporarily from service in the army and placed you at the disposal of this Department for the purpose mentioned in our conferences, I now proceed to give you the instructions by which you are to be guided.
>
> The duty which is proposed to entrust to you is that of a private and confidential agent of this government, for the purpose of proceeding to Ireland, and there using all legitimate means to enlighten the population as to the true nature and character of the contest now waged in this continent, with the view of defeating the attempts made by the agents of the United States to obtain in Ireland recruits for their armies.
>
> It is understood that under the guise of assisting needy persons to emigrate, a regular organization has been formed

of agents in Ireland who leave untried no method of deceiving the laboring population into emigrating for the ostensible purpose of seeking employment in the United States, but really for recruiting the Federal armies.

Throw yourself as much as possible into close communication with the people where the agents of our enemies are at work. Inform them by every means you can devise, of the true purpose of those who seek to induce them to emigrate. Explain to them the nature of the warfare which is carried on here. Picture to them the fate of their unhappy countrymen who have already fallen victims to the arts of the Federals. Relate to them the story of Meagher's Brigade, its formation and its fate. Explain to them that they will be called on to meet Irishmen in battle, and thus to imbrue their hands in the blood of their own friends, and perhaps kinsmen, in a quarrel which does not concern them, and in which all the feelings of a common humanity should induce them to refuse taking part against us.

Contrast the policy of the Federal and Confederate States in former times in their treatment of foreigners, in order to satisfy Irishmen were true sympathy in their favor was found in periods of trial. In the North the Know-Nothing party, based on hatred to foreigners and especially to Catholics, was triumphant in its career. In the South it was crushed, Virginia taking the lead in trampling it underfoot. In this war such has been the hatred of the New England Puritans to Irishmen and Catholics that in several instances the chapels and places of worship of the Irish Catholics have been burnt or shamefully desecrated by the regiments of volunteers from New England. . . . Lay all these matters fully before the people.

If, in order fully to carry out the objects of the Government as above expressed, you should deem it advisable to go to Rome for the purpose of obtaining such sanction from the sovereign pontiff as will strengthen your hands and give efficiency to your action, you are at liberty to do so. . . . You will

receive herewith a letter of introduction to our private agent
in London. . . . You will receive herewith the sum of $1,212.50
in gold, to be applied to the expenses of your voyage and to
your salary.

I am very respectfully, etc.,

J.P. Benjamin,

Secretary of State

Bannon was fit for the task. He felt he could sway the Irish bishops and clergy with stories of abuse of Catholic rituals and sacking
of Catholic churches by the Union soldiers. The truth of the matter, that Bannon intended to wildly exaggerate such instances, was
known only by him. Turning the tide of war by cutting off Irish
recruits to the Union was a mammoth task, but all his life he had
challenged the powerful, conventional wisdom. It was time to do so
again.

A native of Rooskey, County Roscommon, he was the son of a
prosperous grain merchant, James Bannon, who had married Fanny
O'Farrell, the daughter of a very wealthy businessman. John Bannon was born on December 29, 1829. The family opened a corn
brokerage in Dublin and moved to James Street, close to where the
Guinness Storehouse now stands. It was during the wake of Catholic Emancipation, and the Bannon family prospered in the new
business environment that allowed Catholics to own limited property and businesses.

Bannon attended the posh St. Vincent's School in Castleknock
and then studied for the priesthood during the Famine years, which
did not seem to impact the prosperous family. After his ordination
at Maynooth College, he had asked to come to St. Louis, where the
local archbishop was fellow Irishman Peter Kenrick. He had been
a co-founder of Bannon's Irish high school in Dublin some twenty
years earlier, before departing for America. Bannon would have a
joyful reunion.

St. Louis was where 10,000 Irish had decamped after emigrating, and there was a powerful Irish pulse in the city. Church-wise, it

was at the center of the Midwest. Chicago was only eleven years old and a mere stripling; St. Louis was the center of power. For an ambitious young priest, it was a desirable posting.

Father Bannon came from Maynooth in 1853, aged twenty-four, to minister to the large Irish population of St. Louis. The Irish enclave of "Kerry Patch" on the city's north side was a hive of activity, as emigration from Ireland spurred the numbers ever higher. It was still a ghetto, however, where the Irish were segregated from the non-Irish of the city. Most non-Irish St. Louis natives considered it a place to be avoided.

Father Bannon saw the anti-Irish forces at work and became beloved for fighting back. He was eventually assigned to St. John's Parish, a much more middle class area. In November 1860, Bannon's St. John the Apostle and Evangelist Church, a solid brick structure that still stands today, was completed. Then came the Civil War.

After the Civil War began, Bannon's parish in St. Louis was occupied by Union forces, and he fled south where he joined up with the Rebel Irish units, becoming an army chaplain.

If Bannon had stayed in St. Louis, he would very likely have become a bishop. His superior, Archbishop Kenrick, refused to take a position on the war, adhering grimly to a neutral role. We do not know what Bannon thought of slavery, but he certainly did not condemn it, and decided to go with the South with hardly a thought.

Once in the field, though, Bannon was no ordinary chaplain. He knew that chaplains were, in his own words, "frequently objects of derision, always disappearing on the eve of an action, when they would stay behind in some farm house till all was quiet." Bannon took to the field, on one occasion even helping fire a disabled canon. He absolved men from both sides.

Father Bannon later wrote that on nights before major battles, he "would go up to a watch-fire and waking one of the men, call him aside, hear his confession, and send him to summon another. The whole night would be spent thus, in going from campfire to campfire. The men were always willing to come, generally too glad of the opportunity; some would even be watching for me. When the time came for advancing, I made a sign for them all to kneel and gave them absolution. I then went to the second line, or the reserve, till it was their turn also to advance."

Bannon was a heroic figure to Confederate troops. At six foot four with a long bushy beard, he stood out not only for his appearance, but for his bravery, too. General Sterling Price, whose men he served, remarked, "I have no hesitancy in saying that the greatest soldier I ever saw was Father Bannon."

His southern support was in the mainstream of Irish Catholic opinion in the South. The Catholic Church in the South had made its preference known right after the first act of the Civil War, the bombardment and surrender of the Union side at Fort Sumter. The Irish-born Bishop of Charleston, Reverend Patrick Lynch, had a *Te Deum* sung in honor of the great victory and called for all Catholics and Irishmen to enlist on the Confederate side.

Not coincidentally, Bishop Lynch owned eighty-five slaves himself. He authored perhaps the most shameful defense of slavery and the right for white masters to rape female slaves ever by a member of the Catholic hierarchy. He defended flagellation and rape, said slaves enjoyed peace and security in the New World, and said that freed blacks lived idle, dissipated lives and plunged into drunkenness.

In an historical analysis thesis for California State University, Joseph Bell noted that Lynch had excused the rape of young female blacks, saying white men would "seek their gratification whether slavery exist or not." He stated that there was a positive side to this abuse. The fact that black women could be freely raped meant white women would be "exempted from its influence." As a result, he said, "Nowhere in Ireland are white women so pure as (they are) in the South."

Crazy and racist bishops aside, the Scots Irish in the South certainly saw the war differently. They had taken advantage of slavery from the first days they landed in America in 1765. Betty Hutchinson and husband Andrew Jackson, father of the future president, saw emigration to the Carolinas as a way out of penury in Ulster. They left from Carrickfergus in County Antrim.

One recruiting poster for Carolina colonization specifically offered the Irish slavery as a reason to come. One brochure noted that "five healthy negroes" could do all the work on a large plot of land. A letter from a Georgia planter from Northern Ireland stated, "I keep as plentiful a table as most gentlemen in Ireland. . . If any person can bring money to buy a slave or two they may live easy and very well." President Andrew Jackson eventually owned over 150 slaves.

In contrast, few Catholic Irish living in the South at the time of the Civil War owned slaves, having barely enough after the Famine to keep themselves fed and clothed. For those with more prosperous means, the results on owning slaves were more mixed. Irish historian and Civil War expert Damian Shiels has identified six of the top sixteen Confederate officers who were Irish-born as slave holders.

Surprisingly, the main Irish advocate for slavery was John Mitchel, a hero of the abortive 1848 Irish Rising, who had escaped from the harsh confines of Tasmania after transportation and settled in the South. How he reconciled his love for the penniless Irish peasant and his obnoxious and extreme support for slavery has never been properly explained.

Yet, throughout Ireland today there are streets, squares, statues, and football clubs dedicated to Mitchel, an Irish revolutionary of the mid-nineteenth century famous for his newspaper *The United Irishman* and his book "Jail Journal" about his love for Irish freedom and his insistence on the common bond between Irish, Catholic, Protestant, and Dissenter. None of his memorials mention his extreme embrace of slavery.

As for most of the Catholic Irish in the South around the time of the Civil War, they despised the Know-Nothings, the powerful nativist group known for its hatred of Irish Catholics. They had far more traction in the North than in the South, as Secretary of State Judah Benjamin had pointed out in his letter to Bannon.

President Lincoln and his Republican Party were linked to the Know-Nothings, though Lincoln himself adamantly rejected them. There was no doubt, however, that most leading Republican figures were paradoxically anti-slavery and also fiercely anti-Irish Catholic, which was enough for southern Irish to throw in their lot with their neighbors.

The Irish American media also reported the destruction of southern towns and objected strongly to attacks on Catholic churches by anti-Catholic northern troops. In April 1863, there was outrage when a federal regiment from Maine destroyed a Catholic church and brazenly paraded in sacred vestments afterwards. The religious publication *The Tablet* warned that the continued attempts to "plunder, desecrate, and destroy Catholic churches in the south must end."

Besides, even the pope himself was conflicted. His hatred of Garibaldi, who united Italy and sacked the pope from the Vatican, was uppermost in Pope Pius IX's mind. Garibaldi had made clear his pro-Union sympathies and had even offered to lead their army. He had been resident for a time in the United States and was favorably disposed to the Union.

The pope was now back in the Vatican thanks to the French and appeared to tilt towards the Confederacy, partly as a result of Garibaldi's sympathies.

Many Confederates saw the pontiff's support as critical. Catholic France had occupied Mexico and had 40,000 troops on Mexican soil. Could they come to the South's rescue at the pope's command? There was known to be a very large ultramontane streak of absolute fealty to the pope in the French ranks.

Then there was Ireland, with pro-Union recruiters on the ground and the country still in the death grip of post-Famine poverty, exporting 15,000 to 18,000 people a month to America. Could the pope make a direct appeal to the Irish bishops to stop the flow?

Truth was, as the Confederate leadership knew, the Irish recruits were making the difference in the war by sheer weight of numbers, signing up to Union recruiters off the boats in New York Harbor and Boston and points East.

The Union recruiters in Ireland were not worried about how they lured some men into their army. Often, they signed them up for non-existent railroad construction and when the unlucky emigrants found they had been duped, they had little option but to sign up for the army.

Another trick was to fill them full of drink at the harbor in Queenstown and sign them up when they were drunk. It could be a lucrative business; draft dodgers in the United States paid handsomely to have a hapless Irishman signed up in their place.

The shanghaiing of Irish in Ireland and those arriving in America became a national issue, even in Britain.

CHAPTER TWENTY-FOUR

Off the Boat and Into the Arms of the Union

In the summer of 1864, the British parliament heard testimony from, among others, Sir Robert Peel, Chief Secretary for Ireland. He said that between 20,000 and 30,000 Irish had been inveigled into joining up once they landed in America, lured by false promises.

In many cases, Union recruiters in Ireland did the job. Also helping were very poor harvests in the early 1860s due to horrific weather, which drove many to the emigrant boats. Many were people who'd been evicted by their landlords.

The deputy US consul in Dublin, William West, was an enthusiastic supporter of recruiting. As Susannah Bruce describes in her book *The Harp and the Eagle*, West suggested that the US government set aside a plot of land in America to be known as "New Ireland."

He said of "New Ireland," "No doubt General Meagher would in due time be elected Governor if desirably located as to climate, etc. It would be a point d'appui for Irish emigrants, to which they would flock in thousands and thus regenerate themselves in a country and on a soil they could really call their own under a government as free as the air they breathe."

Meanwhile, his senior colleague, the Dublin US Counsel Henry R. Hammond, was worried the Rebels were also recruiting.

In the spring of 1862 he noticed, "There are many Americans in Dublin at this time. Most of them are from the states in rebellion and strange as it may seem there are many here who give an attentive ear to their falsehoods they utter concerning the Rebellion."

So desperate were thousands to escape Ireland, they turned up at the consulates ready to accept free passage in return for enlisting in the US Army. Hammond pushed his government back in the US to allow such a scheme.

The Irish exodus, their ability to fight hard and replace fallen divisions, made them an extremely critical fighting force in the last phase of the war. President Jefferson Davis was aware of this and had surprising Irish contacts himself.

His daughter Winnie had an Irish nanny, Katherine, who had a deep influence on her. Winnie went on to write a biography of Robert Emmet and had as a guest at her eighteenth birthday dinner none other than Oscar Wilde. The Davis housekeeper was Mary O'Melia from Ireland, who stayed with the family through thick and thin. She was the constant companion of Jefferson Davis's wife, Varina.

Mary O'Melia was born Mary Larkin in Galway in 1822. She married Matthew O'Melia, a sea captain, and had three children. Widowed, she came to America and found herself stranded in Virginia visiting when the Civil War began.

Mary ended up running the Confederate White House. She helped Varina dress every morning and arranged the frequent receptions for high-level Confederates at the residence on the corner of 12th and Clay Streets in Richmond. She and Katherine doubtless kept Davis up with the news from Ireland of mass emigration and Union army recruitment.

After Gettysburg and Grant's relentless forcing tactics, Davis was simply running out of men. He knew the Union army was being resupplied every time a shipload of Irish emigrants sailed down the St. Lawrence bound for the East Coast.

They were needed. Grant alone among Lincoln's generals had grasped what the commander-in-chief called the "awful arithmetic"—the side with the greater numbers would eventually win. Jefferson Davis saw it too, hence the summons of Bannon. Stop the Irish and you could possibly stop Grant, too.

Grant believed in "forcing the decisive battle, no matter how brutal," as Adam Gopnik noted in *The New Yorker* review of a recent book simply entitled *Grant,* written by Ron Chernow.

"Robert E. Lee was puzzled why Grant kept forcing men forward after the Battle of Cold Harbor, a seemingly pointless massacre of Union soldiers and heavy casualties on the Rebel side. Lee did not grasp it was Grant's clear tactic, a war of attrition that he with the most soldiers would inevitably win.

"He could lose men and battles of this kind indefinitely and Lee could not," wrote Gopnik. Unlike all the rest of Lincoln's generals, Grant would never turn back or avoid an encounter with the enemy.

Bannon's moment had come. He had been at Vicksburg where General Grant had laid siege and forced a surrender. Vicksburg was the last major Confederate stronghold on the Mississippi River; therefore, capturing it completed the second part of the northern strategy, dividing the southern states and cutting them off from each other. Bannon escaped and made his way to Richmond, the Confederate capitol. It was desperate times; Gettysburg was lost and so was Vicksburg.

In Richmond, Bannon was a man of profound importance and reputation. Navy Secretary Stephen Mallory, the only Catholic in the Confederate cabinet, saw him preach at Sunday Mass and asked him to meet with Jefferson Davis. The meeting occurred on August 30, 1864. It was very rare for Davis to meet lesser officials in person. For those he did entertain, he offered wine and juleps, told war stories from his days on the frontier, and often reminisced about Andrew Jackson, whom he had met as a young boy. With Bannon, however, he was all business.

Davis asked him to go to Ireland to block the recruitment of Irish in whatever way he could. Bannon suggested that he also visit the pope; Davis agreed. Secretary of State Judah Benjamin drew up the necessary papers. There was no doubt the future of the Confederacy could depend on Bannon stopping the flow of Irish recruits. If the pope could be persuaded to back the Confederacy given his hostility towards the Union and their backing for his rival Garibaldi, well, hope might spring again. The French had invaded Mexico and were supportive of the Confederacy. England, too, might look again at diplomatic recognition if the Vatican supported the South. Bannon had a lot riding on his mission.

From the Atlantic port of Wilmington, Father Bannon successfully ran the Union naval blockade aboard a swift blockade runner named the *Robert E. Lee* in early October 1863. Soon after, he arrived in Ireland. His mission had begun.

CHAPTER TWENTY-FIVE

In Ireland, Father Bannon Wins Friends for the Rebels' Cause

Defeat at Gettysburg and Grant's victory at Vicksburg made Father John Bannon's Irish mission even more important. The South had to hold out; their task was easier than Lincoln's. They would win by not losing, eventually forcing secession talks.

After successfully running the Union blockade, Bannon, the Confederate envoy to Ireland, as well as to the pope, headed for London to consult with the Confederacy's ambassador all but in name, Henry Hotze.

Hotze was just reaching his thirtieth birthday, but his youth had not stopped him from becoming the most important Confederate figure in Europe, seemingly with listening posts everywhere.

Hotze gave Bannon ample funds and sent him on his way to proselytize for the Confederacy in Ireland, and to urge the Irish church to call for an end to immigration, given that so many were joining up with the Union army, many unwillingly.

Bannon took up residence at the Angel Hotel on Inns Quay, where Temple Bar, the nightspot hub of Dublin, is now located.

News of Bannon's arrival spread quickly. The Confederate voice had not been heard in Ireland, while on the other side, Thomas Francis Meagher was well known and had spread the Union message.

However, as Bannon's biographer William Barnaby Faherty noted, the horrific toll of Irish lives, especially at Fredericksburg where the Irish Brigade made a suicidal charge, had resulted in William Smith O'Brien, former Young Irelander, compatriot, and fellow escapee from Australia, parting ways with Meagher.

Bannon saw an opening. Dozens of newsmen gathered to hear the Southern story and Bannon was only too happy to oblige.

Bannon stated that Lincoln and his cohorts, the Know-Nothings, swore "No Popery" as loudly as "No Slavery," and that they had invaded the South and destroyed churches and mocked Catholic ritual. The invasion of the South was about Northern capitalists seeking to gain the rich agricultural soil of the South and drive the people off it, he argued, knowing that Famine evictions were very fresh in the minds of the Irish and were still going on.

Bannon supplied newspapers from Southern capitals such as Richmond, which gave a very different view of the conflict. The media hailed his fresh voice and perspective and marveled at his impressive presence. He was six-feet-four inches, handsome, and a marvelous orator.

Bannon adopted several strategies. He adopted the pen name of "Sacerdos," or "Priest," and began hitting the Irish newspapers with articles. Archbishop John McHale, Bishop of Tuam, was an early and influential supporter.

However, Bannon discovered most potential emigrants did not read newspapers and were not highly educated. He quickly made up thousands of posters with the headline "Caution to Immigrants," which were nailed on boarding houses near immigrant departure locations. It was blood-curdling stuff—"Persecution of Catholics in America," "The Tabernacle Overthrown," "Benediction Veil Made a Horse Cover Of," "The Priest Imprisoned and Afterward Exposed on an Island to Alligators and Snakes."

In January 1864, Bannon had twelve thousand posters made up and mailed to every parish priest in Ireland. He called the poster "Address to the Catholic Clergy and People of Ireland."

He wanted to frame the conflict as a religious struggle and an attempt to destroy religion in the South by an Oliver Cromwell called

Abraham Lincoln. Bannon cited numerous outrages, many likely invented, such as Northern invaders burning effigies of the pope, using churches as stables, and kicking around the Blessed Sacrament. The South had long been a haven for Catholics, Bannon argued, and now an attempt was under way to destroy it. In his only ever written reference to slavery, Bannon said the North would make the "Irish lower than the slaves."

Bannon had significant success. The August *London Times* took notice and praised the Irish Confederate priest whose "noiseless industry, devoted zeal, and sound discretion" had so successfully brought about a change to the emigration pattern.

Bannon was a star. Parish priests everywhere wanted him to speak and warn their parishioners off emigration.

Bannon wrote to Judah Benjamin, secretary of state for the Confederacy, quoting an Irish peasant who stated, "We who were all praying for the North . . . would now willingly fight for the South if we could get there." The original Northern tilt was likely heavily influenced by Archbishop Hughes of New York, a towering figure to the Irish clergy.

Bannon felt that seventy-five percent of Irish recruits from Ireland would fight for the South if they could. The *London Times* weighed in again, praising Bannon for the "cogency of the reasoning."

Bannon was joined in Ireland by the slave-holding Bishop of Charleston and Irish native Patrick Lynch. A nephew of Lynch who traveled with him saw Bannon in action as an emigrant ship from Liverpool arrived in Queenstown and about a thousand would-be emigrants were waiting to board.

He reported that the imposing figure of Bannon jumped on a soapbox and delivered a thundering sermon telling them all to go home. Most recognized him and flocked around him.

He told them within four days of arriving in America they'd be flung in jail and given a choice of staying there or joining the army. "My advice to you is return to your homes," he said.

Most present dropped to their knees and asked for Bannon's blessing and then took off back the way they had come, the bishop's nephew reported.

It is estimated that Union recruitment of Irish soldiers dropped by two thirds from December 1863 to July 1864. What would have been the impact if Bannon had arrived in 1861?

Bishop Lynch and Bannon had prearranged to travel to see the pope, who was Pius IX.

Pius was waiting for them, and greeted them warmly. They had a pleasant meeting, but it became clear that a statement of support for the South was not going to happen with the military situation after Vicksburg and Gettysburg swinging so strongly to the North.

Events overtook Bannon exactly as Jefferson Davis had feared. The recruitment of Irish was an important factor, allowing Grant to prevail mainly by sheer weight of numbers.

Bannon would never see America again. Instead, he became a Jesuit, switching orders from being a diocesan priest, and served as a powerful voice for the church in Ireland.

He became Ireland's greatest preacher with thousands showing up for his sermons. He traveled the length and breadth of Ireland, opening missions, fund-raising, and making new friends.

His heart always remained with his beloved South, and towards the end of his life, it was back to the old days around the campfire or galloping to the battlefield to give the last rites to a dying soldier he talked of.

All his life, he kept the letter of instruction from Judah Benjamin, who bizarrely became a practicing barrister in London after barely escaping the Union troops as they went through the South.

Bannon was never held accountable for his acceptance of slavery, and it is extraordinary how he avoided the issue all his life in Ireland.

He also exposed the Catholic Church as an institution that hardly gave slavery a thought when they embraced Bannon. It could not have been that they were ignorant of it. Archbishop McHale's great friend "The Liberator" Daniel O'Connell had called it an abomination repeatedly, yet the church chose not to engage. It must forever remain a stain on the leaders of that generation.

CHAPTER TWENTY-SIX

General Phil Sheridan, the Little Big Fighter

"This Sheridan is a little Irishman but he's a big fighter."
—Abraham Lincoln to Annie Wittenmyer

Of all the Irish men and women Lincoln knew, no one would prove more important to Lincoln in winning the war than "Little Phil"—General Philip Sheridan. Sheridan played a critical role as head of the Union cavalry and later, at age thirty-three, as general of the Army of the Shenandoah, with thirty thousand men under him as Grant closed in on Lee.

During those final weeks, Sheridan was like a whirling dervish, confronting the Confederates at every opportunity. As a strange lassitude and indecision gripped the Union commanders with victory in sight, Sheridan just plunged headlong into every battle he could find.

At one critical point in the closing days of the war, as Grant hesitated on whether to press everything at Lee in a concerted gamble, it was Sheridan who convinced him to go ahead. Sheridan was proven right. For one of the very few times in the Civil War, Grant was in a funk about what to do, and wavering.

Sheridan personally pleaded his case to strike Lee immediately and shook up Grant and his generals, who were prepared to vacillate.

Adam Badeau, a member of the staff of Grant, stated, "Sheridan talked so cheerily, so confidently, so intelligently of what he could do, that his mood was contagious."

A telegram from Lincoln on the matter revealed how much he had come to trust the Irish man. Lincoln sent Grant the telegram on April 7, 1865: "Gen. Sheridan says 'If the thing is pressed I think that Lee will surrender.' Let the thing be pressed."

Lincoln was right to insist. On April 9, 1865, it was Sheridan who blocked Lee's last route of escape from the converging Union armies. Lee had no choice but to surrender at Appomattox Courthouse.

Sheridan, parents from Kilinkeer, County Cavan, had begun the war as a captain and ended up as the fourth-ranked general in the US army after Henry Halleck, Ulysses S. Grant, and William Sherman. It was an incredible rise.

Grant, who had plucked Sheridan from relative obscurity to head up the Union cavalry, was a committed fan. Speaking of Sheridan's abilities, Grant stated that he "ranked Sheridan with Napoleon and Frederick and the great commanders in history"—quite a compliment from the greatest Union soldier of all in the final days of the Civil War.

At the final battle at Five Forks, where vital railway lines to resupply the Confederates were the target, it was Sheridan leading his army who smashed the enemy. Lee had sent an urgent message to General George Pickett to hold Five Forks "at all hazards." His resupply and escape plan could not work if Five Forks was taken.

Sheridan fought like a man possessed. As always, leading from the front, "Little Phil" at one point vaulted from his horse over a Confederate barrier and landed amid thunderstruck enemy soldiers. He ranged up and down the front line shaking his fist at the enemy and urging his men on. Pickett's army collapsed; the final resistance was over, and there was no way out for Lee.

"I believe General Sheridan has no superior as a general, either living or dead, and perhaps not an equal," Grant said, after Five Forks.

For all his greatness, he was deeply controversial. He believed in all-out warfare and a scorched earth policy, whether with Confederate-supporting civilians or later, Indians. His reasoning was clear—war was hell and the sooner it was over with the better, so all available methods were fair.

He was politically brave, too. After the war, as viceroy of Texas, he insisted blacks be allowed to vote as part of reconstruction. President Johnson, in cowardly fashion, removed him because of white outrage.

His was an extraordinary rise. Philip Henry Sheridan was once described by Lincoln as "a brown, chunky little chap, with a long body, short legs, not enough neck to hang him, and such long arms that if his ankles itch he can scratch them without stooping."

Not exactly a ringing endorsement, but like the ungainly Lincoln, it was hardly Sheridan's looks that mattered.

Recalling his meeting on April 4, 1865 with President Lincoln, Sheridan wrote, "I proceeded with General Halleck to the White House to pay my respects to the President. Mr. Lincoln received me very cordially, offering both his Hands, and saying that he hoped I would fulfill the expectations of General Grant in the new command I was about to undertake, adding that thus far the cavalry of the Army of the Potomac had not done all it might have done."

Lincoln's opinion of the hard-driving commander vastly improved with time, and he later said to the Irishman, "General Sheridan, when this particular war began, I thought a cavalryman should be at least six-feet-four inches high, but I have changed my mind. Five feet four will do in a pinch."

The location of Sheridan's birth in 1831 has become a major dispute among Civil War buffs. He claimed he was born in Albany, New York, but there is no record of the family there. Much like famous photographer Matthew Brady, it seems Sheridan preferred to be known as American, given the prejudice against Irish immigrants at the time.

Sheridan family genealogist William Drake has researched Sheridan's birthplace and published his findings on Genealogy.com. He states in part:

> During the last three years of her life, his niece, Nellie Sheridan Wilson, lived with us. Nellie often told me of the General's exploits, before her death in 1947. She regularly mentioned that 'Uncle Phil' was born at sea during the voyage to America... That is what I accept as fact. Sheridan's birth date was March 6, 1831.

Sheridan certainly did not advertise his Irish roots, perhaps because he had presidential ambitions. Civil War historian Damian Shiels turned up a remarkable interview Sheridan gave.

When Sheridan was in Ireland in 1871, he carried out an interview with a Dublin-based correspondent of the *New York Herald*. Sheridan, who was staying in Dublin's Shelbourne Hotel, was asked about Ireland:

> CORRESPONDENT. This, I presume, is your first visit to Ireland?
> GENERAL. My first visit.

> And before I could ask another question the General, turning to the window, which looked out on Stephen's Green—reputed to be the largest square in the world—said, "What a beautiful country." And I must say, that in my heart I fully endorsed his words. The Green, at this season, looks peculiarly beautiful. It is encircled with a row of hawthorns, and interspersed with chestnuts, and as both at this time are putting on their coat of green, and bursting into red and white blossoms, its appearance was most striking and beautiful.

> CORRESPONDENT. Ireland, General, I believe, is the land of your forefathers?

GENERAL. It is; but my family emigrated so long ago that I am unable to say whether it belonged to the north or south. It strikes me it came from Westmeath.

CORRESPONDENT. That is almost in the centre, General, and, although there is great poverty in that district, a magnificent county it is. Have you seen much of Ireland?

GENERAL. Well, yes, a good deal. I have been to Punchestown, and got a good wetting. Both days were fearfully wet. This is a damp climate, I think, and I see that it is raining to-day also. Then, I've been to the north of Ireland for a short time, which appears to me the most nourishing part of the country.

CORRESPONDENT. Belfast is a fine city.

GENERAL. A flourishing city; there's wealth there, and I was greatly pleased with it. It reminded me of an American city. The people are very active, steady and industrious, and I'm sure they'll make great progress. On the whole, I formed a very favorable impression of Ireland and the Irish people.

It is obviously risible that Sheridan could not recall where his parents were from or when his family came to America, given that he was very likely born on the actual boat. It obviously spoke to his desire to not advertise his Irish roots.

While in Dublin, Sheridan turned down a meeting with the Fenian leadership. That was a fact that went down badly back in America, where he explained hastily to Irish American audiences he did support Irish freedom, but he subsequently never spoke out on it. Sheridan had political ambitions, perhaps even the White House. He could not be foreign-born.

Sheridan was a scrapper all his life, being suspended at one point from West Point for a year after getting into a serious physical altercation. He finished in the bottom rung of graduates his year and was posted to several frontier spots in the Oregon territory, where he lived with an Indian mistress. Then the war broke out.

He began the war as a staff member of General Halleck's, but in May 1862, he was promoted to colonel and did so well that General

William Rosecrans promoted him to brigadier general. He was then promoted to major general. The reason was clear. Unlike so many others, Sheridan knew how to fight.

General Grant, who had observed Sheridan's unique leadership ability and utter fearlessness, now called Sheridan to Washington. Grant sent a note to General Halleck, Commander-in-Chief (in name only), that he wanted Sheridan in charge of Shenandoah Valley with an army of thirty thousand to finally cut off the Confederate bread basket and the route they regularly used to attack Northern targets, including Washington.

Grant told the little Irishman, "Give the enemy no rest, do all the damage to railroads and crops you can. Carry off stock of all descriptions, and Negroes, so as to prevent further planting. If the war is to last another year, we want the Shenandoah Valley to remain a barren waste."

The times were growing desperate. Grant's campaign had stalled, and Election Day was drawing nearer. Lincoln needed to remove the threat that Rebels could attack Washington, especially after a raiding party led by Jubal Early almost reached its gates.

Lincoln approved, but Halleck and Secretary of War Stanton disagreed, saying that at just thirty-three, Sheridan was too young for command of an army.

He proved them wrong.

On September 19, he won a small but strategic battle against the Confederate chief tormentor Jubal Early. The stage was set for a final showdown. It was noticeable that men fought better with Sheridan than any other commander. He led from the front, took the same risks and often more risks than they did. Backing down was not in his vocabulary. There was simply no reverse gear.

Sheridan's signal officers had broken the Confederate flagging code, and they passed on a message that Early would be joined by General James Longstreet's army, and that they could crush Sheridan with a surprise attack. It seems Sheridan believed the plan was so risky that it must be fake.

On the night of October 28, the Confederates sprung their attack at Cedar Creek. Sheridan, who had reluctantly gone to Washington at General Halleck's order, was twenty miles away from the fight, woken by the sound of artillery fire in Winchester.

What followed was one of the most dramatic scenes of the Civil War, long remembered in song and story.

Known as "Sheridan's Ride," the event was colorfully described by the man himself.

As he rode out at a furious pace from Winchester, the local ladies, all Confederate followers, began "shaking their skirts at us and were remarkably insolent in their demeanor," he reported.

Sheridan rode on at full lick and several miles from Cedar Creek he encountered his stricken army, fleeing for their lives. "I was assured that all was lost."

But as his men began to recognize him, they took heart and followed him in attacking the enemy. Officers galloped among the fleeing men, telling them Sheridan was now with them. They too turned around, so strong was their confidence in him.

Suddenly the rout was stopped, and Sheridan reformed the battle line and turned it into a dramatic victory.

Sheridan's message that he had sent Early's army "whirling up the valley" soon reached Washington, where it was received with relief and unbridled enthusiasm. Lincoln even gave his employees the day off to celebrate. Re-election suddenly looked much more likely. Confederates would never reach the gates of Washington again.

Irish Phil Sheridan had saved the day.

"Sheridan's Ride," the poem, made him famous for the rest of his life, with every schoolboy and girl in the North able to recite it. A stanza goes:

> The first that the general saw were the groups
> Of stragglers, and then the retreating troops;
> What was done? what to do? a glance told him both,
> Then, striking his spurs, with a terrible oath,
> He dashed down the line 'mid a storm of huzzas,
> And the wave of retreat checked its course there, because
> The sight of the master compelled it to pause.
> With foam and with dust the black charger was gray;

By the flash of his eye, and the red nostrils play,
He seemed to the whole great army to say,
"I have brought you Sheridan all the way
From Winchester, down to save the day."

Grant stated, "Turning what bid fair to be a disaster into glorious triumph stamps Sheridan as . . . one of the ablest of generals."

Sheridan's victory helped Lincoln enormously during the 1864 conventions. As the 1864 election held on November 7 approached, the mood in the country was sour, defeated, and tired of war. Every family was touched by it in some way.

Democrats were in high spirits. Then, the Democratic platform committee allowed a phrase proposed by Clement C. Vallandigham, of Ohio, the phrase being, "The war is a failure."

But that was about to change dramatically as Sheridan and Sherman marched and maneuvered. "The war is a failure" was about to be wrapped around their necks.

Soon after the Democratic convention was over and General George McClellan chosen as candidate, the victories of Sheridan in the Shenandoah Valley and his famous ride to save the day, allied with Sherman's March through Georgia, transformed the mood of the country.

An orator at every major Republican rally picked up the Democratic claim that "the war is a failure" and proceeded to recite "Sheridan 20 miles away," followed by "Marching Through Georgia," which drove audiences wild. Indeed, that infelicitous phrase likely did more than any single thing to give Lincoln a wonderful comeback line and ultimately victory in 1864.

"Little Phil" never looked like a soldier, more like a pint-sized mascot, but he had the heart of a lion.

Sheridan had an often-controversial post-war career. He was brave when supervising federal reconstruction in Louisiana and Texas, where he took an aggressive attitude towards favoring blacks being allowed to vote. He then spent several years in the West directing cavalry operations against Native American tribes.

His use of scorched earth policy and the attribution of the quote, "The only good Indian is a dead Indian," to him (although he denied it), damaged his reputation considerably. He was cold-blooded and murderous in his efforts to destroy the Indians, ordering women and children too to be attacked and tribes pursued even in their winter quarters. One of the men who carried out his orders with undisguised glee was General George Custer, who suffered a catastrophic defeat and lost his life at Little Bighorn.

Sheridan became General-in-Chief of the US Army in 1883 and still held that job when he died of a heart attack age at the age of fifty-seven in 1888. As a fighting man he'd had no equal.

It was a fortunate tide for Lincoln that washed Sheridan and his Irish parents and siblings up on the shores of America in 1831, far from his Cavan roots.

CHAPTER TWENTY-SEVEN

Ford's Theatre—
What Might Have Been

Just six days after Appomattox, Lincoln was shot. Sheridan's boss General Grant stated that the deed was "too horrible to contemplate with composure."

And so the eternal questions will be forever asked: How had it happened? Why was the president not protected properly? Much went back to the events directly prior to the assassination when Lincoln's bodyguard, John Parker, disappeared.

Charlie Forbes would also play a huge role that night, a role that has never been explained. On that dreadful night, the man who drove the Lincoln horse and carriage to Ford's Theatre was Irishman Francis Burke, a controversial figure to this day. Accompanying him as valet was Charlie Forbes, also from Ireland and a Lincoln favorite.

Forbes was a general servant, footman, personal attendant, and occasional driver sometimes charged with looking after Tad Lincoln, the couple's son. He was beloved by the Lincoln family, and was one of the very few Irish that Mrs. Lincoln tolerated.

Old Abe liked kidding his Irish employees, especially Charlie. A story by Tom Pendel, who worked in the White House for thirty-six years, confirms that. On one occasion, President Lincoln, when riding near the Soldiers' Home, said to his footman, named Charles Forbes, who had but recently come from Ireland, "What kind of fruit do you have in Ireland, Charles?" To which Charles replied, "Mr. President, we have a good many kinds of fruit: gooseberries, pears, apples, and the like." The president then asked, "Have you tasted any of our American fruits?"

Charles said he had not, and the president told Burke, the coachman, to drive under a persimmon tree by the roadside. Standing up in the open carriage, he pulled off some of the green (unripe) fruit, giving some of it to Burke and some to Charles, with the advice that the latter try some of it. Charles, taking some of the green fruit in his hand, commenced to eat, when to his astonishment he found that he could hardly open his mouth. Trying his best to spit it out, he yelled, "Mr. President, I am poisoned! I am poisoned!" Mr. Lincoln fairly fell back in his carriage and rolled with laughter.

Forbes would be the footman on the carriage that brought Lincoln to Ford's Theatre on that fateful night of April 14, 1865. Francis Burke would be the driver.

Mary Lincoln wore a black and white striped silk dress and a matching bonnet; Lincoln himself wore a black overcoat and white kid gloves, and carried an Irish linen handkerchief in his pocket. Lincoln's coat was woolen, specially tailored for him by Brooks Brothers of New York. The weather had changed; it was a foggy, misty night.

In an 1892 affidavit, Forbes briefly described his last ever interaction with Lincoln at the White House:

Tad (Lincoln's son) had given me a picture that morning and I still had it in my pocket. . . . When the last visitor had departed and I had helped him on with his great coat, I remembered the picture and said. "Mr. President, Tad gave me a photograph this afternoon and I wish you would put your name on it." "Certainly, Charlie," replied the president and picking up a pen he wrote his name on the photograph and that was the last writing he ever did. For I accompanied him in the carriage, and was with him from the carriage to the theater.

In the same affidavit Forbes, writing twenty-five years after the event, remembered he was in the booth with Lincoln but there is no record of that. He was in the anteroom, which he might have considered was part of the presidential box.

Unlike so many others, Forbes never tried to cash in on his fame as Lincoln's employee, nor did he sell off Lincoln items like other household members did.

Lincoln was also close to his driver, Edward (also called Francis) Burke. When Burke left the White House temporarily on March 4, 1862, Lincoln wrote him a glowing reference and gladly took him back a few years later.

"Edward Burke, the bearer of this, was at service in this Mansion for several months now last past; and during all the time he appeared to me to be a competent, faithful and very genteel man. I take no charge of the servants about the house; but I do not understand that Burke leaves because of any fault or misconduct."

Burke had been in a spot of bother with Lincoln earlier in his administration, refusing a request from the president's staff to fetch Lincoln a newspaper, saying it was not his job.

Incensed, Lincoln himself went out on the street and bought one from a newsboy. The following morning, he ordered Burke to arrive at six a.m. and bring one of Lincoln's sons to fetch the newspaper. Burke learned his lesson.

April 14, 1865 should have been a glorious night for Burke's passenger. "Six hundred thousand Americans had died in the Civil War," James Swanson, who has written two books about Lincoln's death, told NPR. "That war was finally coming to an end. Lincoln had freed the slaves. He had ended secession. There would be no more dying. And Lincoln was filled with joy."

In 1865, Burke gave evidence of his actions on that fateful night.

On April 25, 1865, he gave a statement. It read: "Francis Burns, [sic] the driver of the president's coach, states that on the night of the murder of Mr. Lincoln, he drove him to the theater and stayed at the door until the tragedy occurred. The Special police officer and the footman of the president came up to him to take a drink with them; which he did; but he does not remember anyone else coming up to him in particular, those there were several who asked him questions. He does not know who they were."

The evidence is that Burke, as described, would drop off the presidential party and wait for them to come back at the conclusion of the play.

Burke was described as a big burly Irish coachman who was known to have a fondness for booze, and it is highly unlikely he just had one scoop at the Star Saloon. He was invited to the bar during intermission by the Irish footman Forbes and, unbelievably, John Parker, the police officer who was supposed to be guarding the president's box.

Parker was a complete misfit, previously disciplined for drinking and insubordination. He was once found in a whorehouse while supposedly on duty, and argued the madam had sent for him. He was one of four Washington policeman assigned on a rotating basis to Lincoln, and fate would have it that he was on duty that night. The President of the United States was being solely guarded by a drunk buffoon, who on the night in question was sneaking off to the nearby bar for secret drinks.

Burke, by his own admission, left the carriage and, in the company of "two of my friends," went next door to Peter Taltavull's Star Saloon for an ale. It seems that Forbes and Parker started the drinking session and got Burke to join them. At the trial of conspirator John Surratt in 1867, more than two years after the assassination, there was this exchange between Burke and Defense Attorney Richard Merrick:

MERRICK. Were you on the box most of the night?
BURKE. I was all the time that night, with the exception that two of my friends whom I knew asked me to go in and take a glass of ale with them. I left a man in charge of the carriage until I returned.
MERRICK. At what time did you go in and take a glass of ale?

BURKE. I think after the first act was over.

MERRICK. How long did you remain taking that glass of ale?

BURKE. I suppose about five or ten minutes.

MERRICK. And then returned to the carriage?

BURKE. I then returned to the carriage and went on to the box.

MERRICK. Did you remain there?

BURKE. Yes, sir.

MERRICK. I understand you to say you remained all the time on the box, with the exception of these five or ten minutes.

BURKE. I remained after the carriage first came.

MERRICK. Did you observe anybody coming round your carriage and peeping into it?

BURKE. No; I took no notice. They may have passed by. I saw no one looking into the carriage. I did not see anybody.

MERRICK. You did not go to sleep, did you?

BURKE. Oh, no.

Burke did reveal that his two friends were the "special police officer and the footman of the President." The ill-conceived drinking sessions may have cost Lincoln his life, as Parker should have been on guard when John Wilkes Booth came to hunt down the president.

Earlier that day, Burke had been privy to the last extended conversation between Mary Lincoln and her husband. With the Civil War won, democracy saved, and slavery defeated, Lincoln had wanted to take a celebratory carriage drive.

He told his wife, "I consider this day, the war has come to a close. We must both be more cheerful in the future—between the war and the loss of our darling Willie—we have both, been very miserable." Lincoln told her he wanted to see the Pacific Ocean and perhaps after his second term they would move back to his beloved Illinois. He dreamed of a better future and of no longer sending young men to war.

He had saved the Union, and was hell bent on reconciliation and forgiveness. When crowds in the hundreds of thousands turned up on the White House lawn after Lee's surrender, Lincoln told the band to strike up "Dixie," the Southern anthem. He would heal, not divide.

The fact that he did not live to carry out his plans haunts America even today.

On the fateful night night, Lincoln's party (Burke driving and Forbes seated beside him) arrived at Ford's Theatre at around nine p.m. The play *Our American Cousin* had started. There is strong speculation that the assassin watched the coach arrive to verify the president was present. The orchestra struck up "Hail to the Chief," and a huge standing ovation ensued. There were a thousand people present. Usher James O'Brien escorted the presidential party to the private box.

The star attraction was British actress Laura Keene, who would end up cradling the dying president's bleeding head on her lap. Ironically, it was an Irish play, *The Colleen Bawn*, which had made her famous. Written by Dion Boucicault, it had the longest ever run on the British stage at that time.

She had debuted *My American Cousin,* ironically written by Tony Taylor, a rabid British opponent of Lincoln who later repented, at the eponymous Laura Keene's Theatre in New York in 1858, and was showcasing it in Washington with most of the original cast. Henry Clay Ford, one of three brothers who owned the theater, had been delighted to receive the hand-delivered note from Mrs. Lincoln that she and the president would attend that night—and General Grant too, though he later bowed out.

It was one up for the Fords. Their main rival theater was showing *Aladdin*, full of nineteenth century special effects. Tad Lincoln and his chaperone would attend that show.

The early confirmation allowed the Fords to crank up their PR machine, newsboys and posters displayed all over Washington saying that the president and General Grant, just days after Appomattox, would be present. It was Good Friday, usually a hard day to fill a theater, but not this year. It was also Laura Keene's thousandth performance in the role, a special night for her—and the president would be there!

Lincoln took his seat. The partition between box seven and eight, a wooden construction, had been taken away. The president's rocking chair was ready for him. The lights went down after the ovation and the play continued. The bad days of the Civil War were doubtless on his mind. It had been a very close-run thing, saving this thing called democracy, by the people and for the people

John Parker had been seated as the security outside the box, and then, at intermission, he joined the footman Forbes and coachman Burke in the Star Saloon next door to Ford's Theatre.

John Wilkes Booth was also in the Star Saloon, plucking up Dutch courage. William Withers, the orchestra leader, also nipped out for a drink. He saw Booth "standing at the bar in his shirt sleeves, his coat thrown over one arm." Booth was the first person he met. Withers recalled someone made a joke at Booth's expense. "I remember seeing an inscrutable smile flit across his face and he said, 'When I leave the stage for good, I will be the most famous man in America.'"

He drank whiskey with water and smoked a cigar. He was one of the most famous actors in America, almost every woman fawned over him, and he was a racist through and through. The thought of the death of slavery and the loss of the slave state that secession would have created incensed him.

Booth entered the theater he knew so well shortly after ten. The murder plot was set in motion.

Forbes too was back at his place, sitting inside the anteroom to the presidential box. As the president's valet, he could be called on at any time. The second act began. What Booth saw was Forbes, a thirty-year-old large, hulking Irishman, seated but not blocking the door to the inner vestibule leading to boxes 7 and 8, which had been joined together to make the presidential box.

Booth stopped to speak to Forbes. What they said to each other has never been reported as Forbes was never officially interviewed, which is incredible. What document did Booth use to get past Forbes? Was it a business card or, as some say, a letter? Others say he dropped the name of an influential senator to get access to the box. That scenario would explain why Forbes was never interviewed, or if he was, it was destroyed.

Either way, Forbes, a mere valet, would have recognized the name as that of the famed actor. According to Lincoln historian James Swanson, Forbes had previously admitted a military messenger carrying a dispatch.

Booth was now inside the vestibule leading to the box and was expecting to encounter security, in this case John Parker, the resident bodyguard. But Parker was either still in the Star Saloon or was sitting elsewhere to get a view of the play. It has never been confirmed which. Lincoln was defenseless when the assassin approached.

As for White House doorman Tom Pendel, he claims he warned John Parker to be vigilant as Parker was the sole security agent, tasked with being present when the president arrived and leading him safely into Ford's Theatre.

"John, are you armed?" he asked, before Parker left the White House.

Alphonso Dunn, another doorman and part of the Irish clique, stated, "Oh, Tommy, there is no danger."

Pendel says he replied, "Dunn, you don't know what might happen."

He was right on that. Pendel would stay at the White House thirty-six years and remarkably would witness the aftermath of two more assassinations, President Garfield and President McKinley. It was Lincoln who was on his mind, however, when he sat for a late-life interview. "What a just man was the president," he said—an interesting description of the man who saved the Union.

A fellow presidential bodyguard, William H. Crook, held Parker directly responsible for Lincoln's death. "Had he done his duty, I believe President Lincoln would not have been murdered by Booth," Crook wrote in his memoir. "Parker knew that he had failed in duty. He looked like a convicted criminal the next day."

Crook served twelve presidents and had taken the morning shift on the day Lincoln was assassinated. Eerily, Lincoln told him he had dreamed of being assassinated three successive nights. Crook, worried about his safety, begged him not to go to Ford's Theatre, but Lincoln dismissed his concerns.

After the passing of the president, Burke drove Mrs. Lincoln back to the White House. She was in a bad way, and repeatedly saying "That house, that house," while glaring at Ford's Theatre as they left. Even a stone would have wept for her; she would outlive three of her four sons and her husband in her sad life.

After that night Burke faded into obscurity and is buried in an unmarked grave in Mount Olivet Cemetery in Washington, D.C. Forbes was never interviewed by newspapers about his recollections of the night. He too died, and was placed in an unmarked grave; later, a headstone noting his role with Lincoln was erected. Mary Lincoln wrote him a warm letter afterwards, making clear she did not blame him, and Robert Lincoln employed him when he was Secretary of War.

On November 12, 1983, Irish Ambassador Tadgh O'Sullivan officially unveiled a new tombstone over the Forbes grave, noting his role with the Lincoln family at the Congressional Graveyard in Washington. A color guard was present.

But the question will always loom: What did Booth say to Forbes to gain entrance to the presidential box that night? In the end, the Irishman was Lincoln's last line of defense, but he was his valet, not his bodyguard. Charlie Forbes brought many secrets to the grave with him.

Secretary of War Edwin Stanton decided he wanted the crime scene photographed exactly as it was the moment Lincoln was shot. He called in Irish photographer Matthew Brady to take photographs of the interior of the theater, then the exterior of the president's box and the approach to the box and the anteroom. Brady had to use all his skill in the dimly lit theater.

It was a far cry from the triumphant days when he had photographed the aesthetically challenged candidate Lincoln in February 1860 and "photoshopped" him so well that Lincoln gave him much credit for winning the White House.

CHAPTER TWENTY-EIGHT

The Co-Conspirators —A Catholic Plot?

Robert Redford's 2011 movie *The Conspirator* takes a close look at the assassination and trial of the conspirators who hatched the plot to kill Lincoln.

At the center of Redford's movie, in fact, is Mary Surratt (played by Robin Wright), who was accused of participating in the plot to kill Lincoln and assist Booth's escape. The plotters also met at her place.

Much was made, in the frenzy following Lincoln's assassination, of Surratt's religion. She was a devout Roman Catholic at a time when the religion itself was hated by millions.

As historian Tom Deignan has noted, "Surratt as well as her accused son, John, were [both] Catholic. [A] man with the name of O'Laughlin [was also] among those accused of taking part in the plot to kill Lincoln. It should be no surprise that a conspiracy theory swiftly took hold that Catholics were at the center of the plot to kill Lincoln."

Incredibly, to this day, the Internet is filled with conspiracy theories outlining the Vatican's role in killing Lincoln, not to mention the Jesuits.

An ex-priest who Lincoln had once defended in court, named Charles Chiniquy, once stated that, when it came to killing the American president, "the Jesuits alone could select the assassins, train them, and show them a crown of glory in heaven."

Even Booth may have converted to Catholicism. His sister thought so and he had a Catholic medal on his person when shot.

O'Laughlin did play a role in an earlier attempt to kidnap the president, though his religious background has been under debate for years, with some believing he was Catholic, while others arguing that he was actually Methodist.

John Surratt, for one, had planned on becoming a priest, had met with Booth to plan to kidnap Lincoln on March 17 (St. Patrick's Day!) of 1865, and even fled to Rome after Booth killed the president.

Either way, the Catholic plot was one of the "fake news" stories that surfaced soon after the president's death.

CHAPTER TWENTY-NINE

Irishmen Seeking the Killer Booth

The longest-living survivor present at Lincoln's assassination, Samuel Seymour, died in 1956 at age ninety-six. He was a five-year-old boy brought to the theater on a trip to Washington from Maryland by his godmother. He remembered vividly the moment he saw Lincoln.

"When he finally did come in, she (his godmother) lifted me high so I could see. He was a tall, stern-looking man. . . . He was smiling and waving to the crowd.

"Everyone sat down again. All of a sudden, a shot rang out and someone in the president's box screamed. I saw Lincoln slump forward in his seat. . . . I thought there had been another accident when one man seemed to tumble over the balcony rail and land on the stage."

Lincoln was rushed from the theater across the street to William Petersen's Boarding House. There, an Irishman immediately took charge, ensuring order and giving the doctors ample space and time to do their work.

James O'Beirne, from Roscommon, was the Provost Marshal of Washington, D.C., a job that put him in charge of the military police. It meant he would be one of those heading up the pursuit of the conspirators, especially Booth.

Years later, he remembered his experience:

I was officially present as provost marshal of the District of
Columbia . . . where the great Lincoln lay on his deathbed
from the time when he was first carried into the modest house
where he died on Tenth Street nearly opposite Ford's Theatre,
in Washington. I was at Secretary Stanton's side and stood
near him at the rear door in the gray of the morning when Mr.
Lincoln died.

He had been unconscious, manifesting life only by heavy
stertorous breathing from the moment when he was first laid
in the little rear bed chamber where he died.

When first brought through he was more than comatose,
hardly breathing. At the suggestion of a physician, a civilian
then in charge of him ran to the restaurant next door to the
theater and procured a large sarsaparilla glass of brandy,
which was poured down Mr. Lincoln's throat and seemed to
establish respiration.

O'Beirne remembered it vividly. "When Mr. Lincoln breathed his
last in a guttural, gassing struggle for breath, Mr. Stanton was looking out the window into the breaking twilight of morning dawn."

Stanton directed him to go to the Kirkwood Hotel to secure Vice
President Johnson, who was staying there. Johnson had an amazing
story to tell. All night in the room upstairs, he and his Negro servant
heard coming and going and slamming doors.

The room had been rented by George Atzerodt, the conspirator
charged with killing Vice President Johnson. However, Atzerodt had
backed out at the last moment. O'Beirne ordered the room searched,
and vital clues were found, including a revolver and ammunition
probably meant to kill Johnson.

O'Beirne was now officially on the trail of Booth.

O'Beirne was a hero and a Medal of Honor winner. He was
born in Roscommon in September 1842. His parents were Michael

O'Beirne and Eliza Rowan. His father was affiliated with the Young Islanders and knew Thomas Francis Meagher.

The family emigrated to New York when he was a young boy. He earned a Master of Arts degree from St. John's University and went to work for his father after graduation.

When the Civil War broke out, he enlisted with the regiment known as the Irish Rifles after his tour with another company was up.

At the Battle of Fair Oaks, he displayed such bravery that he was awarded the Medal of Honor. He was badly injured at Chancellorsville and invalided out.

Secretary of War Stanton wrote to him officially and said, "Major O'Beirne you are relieved from all other duties at this time and directed to deploy yourself . . . in the [pursuit] of the murderers of the president."

That was exactly what O'Beirne would do. He had loved the president and wanted to catch his killer at all costs. He would be joined by another Irishman who also proved vital to the quest. It would be the biggest manhunt in American history.

O'Beirne's search went cold in Virginia. At one point he was within ten miles of where Booth was hiding out. He did share in the reward money, an acknowledgement of his efforts. It was another Irishman who would gain a huge measure of fame.

CHAPTER THIRTY

Edward Doherty Gets His Man

Edward P. Doherty was born September 26, 1838, in Wickham, Canada East, to immigrant parents from County Sligo.

He moved to New York in 1860 and enlisted with the 71st New York volunteers and was captured by the Confederates but made a bold escape.

Doherty went on to become a captain in the Corcoran Legion, formed by fellow prisoner from the First Battle of Bull Run, Irish American General Michael Corcoran. Doherty served for two years before being appointed First Lieutenant in the 16th New York Cavalry on September 12, 1863. The regiment was assigned to the defense of Washington, D.C. for the duration of the war, where Doherty distinguished himself as an officer.

On the afternoon of April 24, Lieutenant Doherty was seated on a bench in a park opposite the White House enjoying the spring day. His unit was protecting Washington, and the pursuit of Booth was far from his mind.

A messenger suddenly approached him with an urgent call to action. The letter was from Doherty's superior. It demanded he recruit twenty-five men and report to Colonel Baker.

Doherty leaped to his feet and sprinted back to his barrack and had the bugler play "Boots and Saddles," the call-out signal to his unit. He took the first twenty-six men and quickly arranged a meeting with Colonel Baker.

Baker showed him a photograph of who they were pursuing—John Wilkes Booth. Corcoran could feel the rising excitement—he was helping lead the biggest manhunt in history.

Two detectives would accompany them, Luther Baker and Everton Conger. By that evening, they were on their way. They boarded a ferry to Virginia and arrived close to the last point where Booth had been sighted. They were all keenly aware of the $100,000 reward, which would be close to $1.5 million today.

Booth fled south on horseback and, after meeting with one of his co-conspirators, David Herold, picked up supplies from a Maryland inn run by Mary Surratt. With his broken leg severely impacting his progress and in dire need of medical attention, Booth and Herold went to the house of a Dr. Samuel Mudd to have his leg set.

After Mudd ordered them off his property, they were briefly helped by a variety of Confederate soldiers and sympathizers as they headed to Virginia. Once across the Potomac, they sought refuge in a barn on the farm of Richard Garrett.

It was there, almost two weeks after Lincoln was shot, that Union soldiers of the 16th New York Cavalry found Booth and Herold.

The following is Lt. Edward P. Doherty's account of what happened, which Eyewitness History adapted from an article Doherty wrote for *Century Magazine* in 1890, titled "Pursuit and Death of John Wilkes Booth":

Lt. Doherty himself from an updated 1890 interview by Eyewitness History tells history.

The Account of the Officer in Charge. Scouring the countryside around the Rappahannock River, Doherty is told the two fugitives were last seen at a farm owned by Richard Garrett. Doherty leads his squad to the farm arriving in the early morning hours of April 26.

I dismounted, and knocked loudly at the front door. Old Mr. Garrett came out. I seized him, and asked him where the men were who had gone to the woods when the cavalry passed the previous afternoon. While I was speaking with him some of the men had entered the house to search it. Soon one of the soldiers sang out, "Oh Lieutenant! I have a man here I found in the corn-crib." It was young Garrett, and I demanded the whereabouts of the fugitives. He replied, "In the barn." Leaving a few men around the house, we proceeded in the direction of the barn, which we surrounded. I kicked on the door of the barn several times without receiving a reply. Meantime another son of Garrett's had been captured. The barn was secured with a padlock, and young Garrett carried the key. I unlocked the door, and again summoned the inmates of the building to surrender.

After some delay Booth said, "For whom do you take me?"

I replied, "It doesn't make any difference. Come out."

He said, "I am a cripple and alone."

I said, "I know who is with you, and you had better surrender."

He replied, "I may be taken by my friends, but not by my foes."

I said, "If you don't come out, I'll burn the building." I directed a corporal to pile up some hay in a crack in the wall of the barn and set the building on fire.

As the corporal was picking up the hay and brush, Booth said, "If you come back here I will put a bullet through you."

I then motioned to the corporal to desist, and decided to wait for daylight and then to enter the barn by both doors and overpower the assassins.

Booth then said in a drawling voice, "Oh Captain! There is a man here who wants to surrender awful bad."

I replied, "You had better follow his example and come out."

His answer was, "No, I have not made up my mind; but draw your men up fifty paces off and give me a chance for my life."

I told him I had not come to fight; that I had fifty men, and could take him.

Then he said, "Well, my brave boys, prepare me a stretcher, and place another stain on our glorious banner."

At this moment Herold reached the door. I asked him to hand out his arms; he replied that he had none. I told him I knew exactly what weapons he had.

Booth replied, "I own all the arms, and may have to use them on you, gentlemen."

I then said to Herold "Let me see your hands." He put them through the partly opened door and I seized him by the wrists. I handed him over to a non-commissioned officer. Just at this moment I heard a shot, and thought Booth had shot himself. Throwing open the door, I saw that the straw and hay behind Booth were on fire. He was half-turning towards it.

He had a crutch, and he held a carbine in his hand. I rushed into the burning barn, followed by my men, and as he was falling caught him under the arms and pulled him out of the barn. The burning building becoming too hot, I had him carried to the veranda of Garrett's house.

Booth received his death-shot in this manner. While I was taking Herold out of the barn one of the detectives went to the rear, and pulling out some protruding straw set fire to it. I had placed Sergeant Boston Corbett at a large crack in the side of the barn, and he, seeing by the igniting hay that Booth was leveling his carbine at either Harold or myself, fired, to disable him in the arm; but Booth making a sudden move, the aim erred, and the bullet struck Booth in the back of the head, about an inch below the spot where his shot had entered the head of Mr. Lincoln. Booth asked me by signs to raise his hands. I lifted them up and he gasped, "Useless, useless!" We gave him brandy and water, but he could not swallow it. I sent to Port Royal for a physician, who could do nothing when he came, and at seven o'clock Booth breathed his last. He had on his person a diary, a large bowie knife, two pistols, a compass, and a draft on Canada for sixty pounds.

Doherty may have embellished his role, as did all the other major participants in the hunting down of John Wilkes Booth. The reward money was huge and the fight for the blood money was ferocious, eventually ending in a congressional investigation into how the money was distributed.

In the end, the assassin got what he deserved, a bullet to the head very similar to the location of the shot he fired to kill the president.

The bullet was fired by one of the strangest characters in American history, an Englishman of Irish heritage known as Boston Corbett who came to America and discovered old-time religion after living like a tramp. Ashamed of his sexual desires after he converted, he castrated himself by removing his testicles with a knife.

Despite his bizarre actions, Corbett was a good soldier. As the barn was set ablaze, he saw through a crack that Booth was preparing to come out shooting. He aimed carefully and took him down with a single shot. Booth had died like he wanted, alone, dramatically ready to come out with guns blazing.

The instruction had been to bring back Booth alive, so there was initial consternation as the issue of his co-conspirators was a vital one. In time, however, Boston Corbett was seen to have been justified. Booth would have taken as many soldiers as he could down in his version of a glorious death.

The manhunt was over.

As for Doherty, he returned a hero and got his share of the reward, which was $52,550 when shared out among all the men on the manhunt. He was promoted to captain and stayed in the regular army until mustering out in 1871. He moved to New Orleans for a time, before returning to New York where he became an inspector in the street paving department. He was Grand Marshal of the New York Memorial Day parade and eventually retired in New York. He was buried in Arlington Cemetery after passing away in 1897.

However his ancestral hometown in Sligo did not forget him, nor did a mysterious military figure. There is a grave to family members in Sligo and a tombstone inscription, which reads:

> In the beloved memory of Elizabeth Crawford Gribbin, first love and wife of Henry Doherty Esq. and their son Joseph and his sons Michael, Colonel Henry J. Doherty, and Captain Edward P. Doherty, The Brave Avenger of President Lincoln and their youngest daughter Catherine Tresa and to the memory of their eldest daughter Mary Anne Doherty who in fond remembrance has erected this monument in the year 1887.

The "Brave Avenger" line was added by a mysterious General Kavanagh from America, who secured family permission. Many Americans visit the graveyard seeking relatives and are delighted at the West of Ireland connection to Lincoln.

Borough Council graveyard employee, Brian Scanlon, told the Irish Independent newspaper that the cemetery attracts many US tourists:

> They don't ask about the Lincoln connection. They call in, mainly during the summer, enquiring about their ancestors.
>
> I show them around and I often bring them to the Doherty grave and they're delighted. They don't expect to see such a strong connection in Sligo in the West of Ireland to Lincoln.

Though buried in Arlington, Doherty has not been forgotten in his family's native heath.

CHAPTER THIRTY-ONE

Lincoln and the Irish— Linked Forever

In the end, America lost its greatest president, a man who saved the fragile flower of a democracy still much less than 100 years old when the Civil War broke out. At its greatest hour of need he was there, never wavering despite lesser voices chanting for conciliation with the South and change. His absence during the Reconstruction meant unfinished business on race, which continues to this day.

At the Hampton Roads peace parley with Southern representatives in 1865, he was at his very best, demanding military surrender rather than a peace treaty that would allow wiggle room on slavery.

He was immediately adamant that slavery must go, and he kicked the underpinnings of it from underneath them forever by ridiculing the Southern leadership's inane view that slavery was good for black folk too, as they were less intelligent.

His political skills were incredible, and his physical presence at six foot four, probably six foot seven with a stovepipe hat on, must have overwhelmed and dwarfed his opponents. His ability to relax people with his backwoods stories and an occasional Irish joke was legendary. His sense of mercy and conciliation registers far greater today, when we see so little of it practiced.

After his death, there was talk of the South rising again but it was General Robert E. Lee who put an end to that. He had come around in the end to the belief that nothing more was to be gained by restarting the murderous battle. Six hundred thirty thousand dead were more than enough.

Many were Irishmen, and Lincoln made clear in his dealings with Thomas Francis Meagher, Michael Corcoran, and Archbishop Hughes that he was indeed grateful. General Philip Sheridan had also played a huge role.

But so too had the 150,000 Irish who fought for the Union. The war was simply not winnable without them.

Lincoln stayed true to the Irish; as an utter outsider himself, that sense of the underdog likely drew him to the Irish. His own staffers complained about the "Mick Clique" around him, but he clearly reveled in the laughter and the country stories. He cared about their issues, supporting Famine relief when he was an unknown politician and ensuring their cause of Irish freedom was raised in Congress.

Lincoln's embrace of the despised Irish should never be overlooked, nor their role in helping him win one of the most important conflicts of all times, which, with a different outcome, would have transformed the world we live in even today.

Lincoln's greatness is never in question. Robert Lincoln O'Brien, writing in 1914 in the *Boston Globe*, summed up Lincoln and his meaning well:

More than a million people a year now pour into the United States from lands beyond the seas, most of them unfamiliar with our language and our customs and our aims. When we Americans who are older by a few generations go out to meet them we take, as the supreme example of what we mean by our great experiment, the life of Abraham Lincoln. And, when we are ourselves tempted in the mad complexity of our material civilization to disregard the pristine ideals of the republic, we see his gaunt figure standing before us and his outstretched arm pointing to the straighter and simpler path of righteousness. For he was a liberator of men in bondage, he was a savior of his country, he was a bright and shining light.

As for the revisionist view that he could have avoided a war, his words to Irish American judge Joe Gillespie, a close friend, shortly before he took over from Buchanan, ring true: "It is only possible upon(with) the consent of this Government to the erection of a foreign slave government out of the present Slave States."

Lincoln was never going to allow that, but it was a close-run thing. The Irish contribution to the success has long been underplayed, even down to the present day. Many came off the Famine ships and went to war for the Union and Lincoln. Even in Union ranks they sometimes faced hostility from men like General William Sherman. But they persevered. Archbishop Hughes told them the Union and Lincoln was everything to fight for, as did their heroes. One of their own, Philip Sheridan, was the bravest general in the war. Lincoln had kissed the Irish flag and stated, "God Bless the Irish."

So they fought. *Fág an Bealach*, which translates as "Clear the Way"—the old Irish war cry rings true for the American Civil War and the Irish contribution. The Irish helped enormously to "clear the way" for a deeply embattled president who ended up as America's greatest leader. They deserve proper recognition for that.

Kennedy Retraces Lincoln and Gettysburg

John F. Kennedy was fond of invoking Republican Abe Lincoln in his speeches. To those who disagreed with his Lincoln homages, he said, "Some may say that a Democratic candidate for the Presidency has no right to invoke the name of Lincoln. I disagree. Abraham Lincoln belongs to the ages, and he belongs to all Americans, regardless of their party."

Kennedy undertook a pilgrimage to Gettysburg as president to pay such a homage. On Saturday March 31, 1963, Kennedy, dressed in a blue jacket and driving a white Mercury convertible with the top down, headed a five-car convoy, which included four Secret Service cars, from Camp David to the Gettysburg battlefield, a distance of 26.2 miles.

It had been almost one hundred years since Lincoln's Gettysburg Address, and Kennedy doubtless felt he could be back again in November to deliver a speech marking that momentous anniversary.

Accompanying him was his wife Jackie and oldest child Caroline, both of whom sat in the front seat. In the back was Red Fay, his Undersecretary of the Navy, but more importantly, a reliable Kennedy sidekick and later author of a fawning memoir about Kennedy called *The Pleasure of His Company*.

Fay later recounted the visit. Along the way, they picked up local high school teacher and Gettysburg expert Jacob Sheads, who met the presidential party in a parking lot near the site of the battle and was astonished to find the president behind the wheel of his own car.

There may not have been much need for Sheads, as Fay recalled. "The knowledge the president displayed about the Civil War amazed me. When we came to a certain area where a Boston or Massachusetts unit had fought, he recounted the battle with such detail I could almost see it taking place. I kept expecting a Kelly or a Murphy to come charging up the gorge."

Sheads thought his well-planned itinerary would please the president, but JFK had other ideas, displaying his knowledge of the battlefield in such a manner that it drew Sheads's admiration.

After visits to several landmarks, Kennedy then drove to Rose's Wheatfield, through which the Irish Brigade had charged on July 2, 1863, suffering grievous losses. The monument to the Irish brigade is on top of the Stony Hill/Loop area of the battlefield. Nearby is a monument to the Massachusetts 28th, an all-Irish regiment. On top of the monument is inscribed the Fenian battle cry "*Fág an Bealach*." The guide asked Kennedy if he understood the words; Kennedy answered instantly, "Clear the Way." Sheads realized that this was a man who knew his Irish American history.

There is even video of Kennedy, taken by Deborah Deitsch Mason, a relative of Sheads. In it, Jack and Jackie are close together in the front seat, and he is pointing out landmarks. Poignantly, they are near the Eternal Light Peace Memorial. Sheads would later say that Jackie Kennedy got the idea for the eternal flame over her husband's grave from the Eternal Light Peace Memorial at Gettysburg.

Lincoln and Kennedy had many similarities. Both were avatars of a new age, both magnificent orators and inspirational examples for their fellow citizens. Both took on the battle for the rights of the widely despised black Americans. Both would die at the zenith of their careers from an assassin's bullet.

JFK even cribbed a few words from Lincoln in his inauguration on January 20, 1960:

"In your hands, my dissatisfied fellow-countrymen, and not in mine, is the momentous issue of civil war." [From Abraham Lincoln's first inaugural address, March 4, 1861]

"In your hands, my fellow citizens, more than mine, will rest the final success or failure of our course." [From John F. Kennedy's inaugural address]

On that March day in 1963, their paths also crossed, the Irish American descendant of Famine emigrants and the country lawyer from Springfield. They both owed a great debt to the Irish: Kennedy, for helping elect him by voting in massive numbers, and Lincoln, for their role in helping him win the Civil War. Lincoln, although initially thinking of the Irish as foes of the Democratic Party, embraced them in the end as they embraced him, despite their fears of his alleged links to the nativist Know-Nothings.

As for Kennedy, the Irish in the Civil War entranced him. Before the president's visit to Ireland in June 1963, Letitia Baldrige Hollensteiner, the White House Social Secretary, remembers how determined Kennedy was to remind his ancestral countrymen of the importance of that involvement. She later wrote:

I once found an old flag, an Irish Brigade flag which had been used during the Civil War by the Irish Brigade here in this country. He liked that very much, and we got it to give to the President of Ireland. He and Mrs. Kennedy spent a great deal of time deciding how it should be presented; how it should be framed, encased in glass, what the plaque should say. The President, being such an historian, insisted that the plaque tell the whole story of the flag. He made me check and recheck, and he said, 'That sounds fishy. Something's wrong with your facts. Get your facts straight.'

There was one more moment of communion between the two most charismatic presidents. After JFK's assassination, Jackie Kennedy immediately decreed that Lincoln's funeral be the lodestar for her husband's obsequies.

Historians quickly studied how the White House had been enveloped in black in mourning for Lincoln, and the order of the funeral, such as who marched where and when, was also studied. One last-minute request Jackie made was for an eternal flame beside the grave. She said she wanted to light a flame at the climax of the service in Arlington that would burn forever in memory of her husband.

She remembered the day when she and the president had visited Gettysburg. There, at the Eternal Light Peace Memorial, dedicated in 1938, she had seen an eternal flame. A similar one was built in Arlington over his freshly-dug grave in time for Jackie to light it on Monday afternoon. A final connection was made between two tragic presidents—one who had dared to dream and another to fight for the dream of democracy when it came to it.

BIBLIOGRAPHY

Baker, Jean H. *Mary Todd Lincoln*. New York: W.W. Norton, 2008.

Barnaby Faherty S.J., William. *Exile in Erin: A Confederate Chaplain's Story*. St. Louis: Missouri History Museum Press, 2002.

Brands, H.W. *The Man Who Saved the Union: Ulysses Grant in War and Peace*. New York: Anchor Books, 2013.

Bruce, Susannah Ural. *The Harp and The Eagle: Irish-American Volunteers and the Union Army*. New York: New York University Press, 2006.

Chernow, Ron. *Grant*. New York: Penguin Press, 2017.

Corby, William, C.S.C., Edited by Lawrence Francis Kohl. *Memoirs of Chaplin Life: 3 Years in the Irish Brigade with the Army of the Potomac*. New York: Fordham University Press, 1992.

Egan, Timothy. *Immortal Irishman*. New York: Houghton Mifflin Harcourt, 2016.

Fay Jr., Paul B. *The Pleasure of His Company*. New York: Dell Books, 1967.

Goodwin, Doris Kearns. *Team of Rivals: The Political Genius of Abraham Lincoln*. New York: Simon and Schuster, 2006.

Gottfried, Bradley M. *Stopping Pickett: The History of the Philadelphia Brigade*. Shippensburg, PA: White Mane Publishing, 1999.

Gynne, S.C. *Rebel Yell: The Violence, Passion, and Redemption of Stonewall Jackson*. New York: Scribner, 2014.

Headley, Joel Tyler. *Great Riots of New York: 1712–1873*. New York: Thunder's Mouth Press, 2003.

Herndon, William H. *Herndon's Life of Lincoln*. Rockville, Maryland: Wildside Press, 2008.

Korda, Michael. *Clouds of Glory: The Life and Legend of Robert E. Lee*. New York: Harper Collins, 2014.

Pendel, Thomas. *36 Years In The White House*. Sagwan Press, 2015.

Pinsker, Matthew. *Lincoln's Sanctuary*. Oxford: Oxford University Press, 2005.

Sars, Stephen. *The Landscape Turned Red: The Battle of Antietam*. Boston: Ticknor & Fields, 1983.

Sears, Stephen. *Gettysburg*. New York: Houghton Mifflin Harcourt, 2003.

Shiels, Damian. *Irish in the American Civil War*. Stroud, UK: The History Press, 2014.

Shiels, Damian. *The Forgotten Irish*. Stroud, UK: The History Press, 2017.

Silverman, Jason H. *Lincoln and the Immigrant*. Carbondale, IL: Southern Illinois University Press, 2015.

Stoddard, William O. *Lincoln's Third Secretary: The Memoirs of William O. Stoddard*. New York: Exposition Press, 1955.

Swanson, James L. *Manhunt: The 12-Day Chase for Lincoln's Killer*. New York: William Morrow, 2006.

Thomas, Benjamin J. *Abraham Lincoln*. New York: Barnes & Noble Books, 1994.

Tucker, Phillip Thomas. *Pickett's Charge: A New Look at Gettysburg's Final Attack*. New York: Skyhorse Publishing, 2016.

INDEX

Photo Credit: Fergus O'Dowd

ABOUT THE AUTHOR

Niall O'Dowd is a native of Ireland who emigrated to America in 1979. He is founder of the *Irish Voice* newspaper, *Irish America* magazine, and IrishCentral.com, the largest Irish Diaspora site. He was awarded an honorary doctorate degree from University College Dublin and the Irish Presidential Distinguished Services Award for his role in the Irish peace process. His previous books include *Fire in the Morning*, about the Irish heroes of 9/11, and *An Irish Voice*, a memoir. In March 2018, he will be named as one of the ten most influential Irish-born people who came to America. He is the only current-day nominee.